STEROIDS

Big Muscles, Big Problems

Alvin, Virginia,
and Robert Silverstein

—Issues in Focus—

ENSLOW PUBLISHERS, INC.

Bloy St. and Ramsey Ave.
Box 777
Hillside, N.J. 07205
U.S.A.

P.O. Box 38
Aldershot
Hants GU12 6BP
U.K.

Library of Congress Cataloging-in-Publication Data

Silverstein, Alvin.
　Steroids: big muscles, big problems/Alvin, Virginia and Robert
Silverstein.
　　　p. cm.—(Issues in focus)
　Includes bibliographical references and index.
　Summary: Discusses the reasons why athletes and others use
steroids and some of the problems associated with these drugs.
　ISBN 0-89490-318-7
　1. Doping in sports—Juvenile literature. 2. Anabolic steroids—
Health aspects—Juvenile literature. [1. Steroids. 2. Athletes—
Drug use. 3. Drug abuse.] I. Silverstein, Virginia B.
II. Silverstein, Robert A. III. Title. IV. Series: Issues in focus
(Hillside, N.J.)
RC1230.S55　1992
362.29—dc20　　　　　　　　　　　　　　　91-876
　　　　　　　　　　　　　　　　　　　CIP
　　　　　　　　　　　　　　　　　　　AC

Printed in the United States of America

10 9 8 7 6 5 4

Illustration credits:
The Bettmann Archive, pp. 8, 27, 62, 64, 79, 84, 98; *Courier-News* photo,
courtesy of Robert Allen, p. 93; Dick Locher, Tribune Media Services, pp. 60, 76;
By permission of Doug Marlette and Creators Syndicate, p. 21; Food and Drug
Administration, p. 43; By permission of Johnny Hart and NAS, Inc., p. 34; Larry
Alpaugh, Tewksbury Photographers, pp. 23, 89; Illustration by Mike Scott for the
Courier-News, p. 39; Steve Moore, Tribune Media Services, p. 46; U.S. Depart-
ment of Education, p. 56.

Cover Illustration:
AP/Wide World Photos

Acknowledgments

The authors would like to thank Dr. Harrison G. Pope, Jr., of Harvard Medical School for his careful reading of the manuscript and his helpful comments, suggestions, and encouragement.

***

In the listings of references at the ends of the chapters, we have tried to emphasize sources whose importance, depth of coverage, and reading level would merit a further look by readers interested in particular areas. They represent only a fraction of the hundreds of articles, pamphlets, and books (many of them highly technical) that the authors consulted in writing this book.

Contents

1

The Steroid Epidemic

What is the number one problem in the United States today? According to opinion polls, Americans are most worried about drugs. The drugs they have in mind are crack, cocaine, and marijuana. But some experts believe the nation is faced with an even bigger drug problem. Philadelphia physical therapist Pat Croce says, "People think the cocaine issue is big. It's not as big as anabolic steroids. Among kids it's epidemic."

Steroids have been in the news a lot lately. Until a few years ago, though, only doctors and athletes had even heard of the word. There were occasional reports about football players or bodybuilders using steroids, but these drugs didn't hit the headlines until the 1988 Olympics. Canadian sprinter Ben Johnson set a new world record for the 100-meter dash on September 24, covering the distance in just 9.79 seconds to win the race. Three days later the world's excitement turned to shock when the International Olympic Committee announced that tests of Johnson's urine had showed traced of stanozolol, an anabolic steroid. The runner's victory and gold medal were taken away, and he

A positive test for steroid use wiped out Ben Johnson's Olympic win and world record.

went home in disgrace, suspended from international competition for two years and banned from the Canadian team for life.

Even before the 1988 Olympic scandal, most experts knew that steroids were being widely used in sports. Some studies estimated that up to 80 percent of professional football players, half of all world-class athletes, and 20 percent of college and high school athletes used steroids to help them perform better. It was assumed that about one million Americans were taking steroids—most of them athletes and bodybuilders.

A startling study released at the end of 1988 revealed that the steroid problem was far more serious than anyone had suspected. William Buckley and Charles Yesalis of Pennsylvania State University reported that 6.6 percent of 3,403 high school seniors, surveyed at forty-six high schools across the nation, had used or were still using steroids. If that sample was representative of the whole country, as many as 500,000 American high school students were present or former steroid users! Many of them were taking the drugs to try to improve their performance in sports, but others were not even involved in athletics. Recent studies have revealed even more alarming facts. Experts are finding that eleven- and twelve-year-old boys are experimenting with steroids, and girls are trying them, too.

The "steroids" that are now making headlines as drugs of abuse are synthetic variations of a group of natural chemicals that play many powerful and important roles in the body. Some synthetic steroids come in pill form; others are injected with a needle. Many people who take steroids take several different kinds at once. The use of these drugs is illegal unless they are prescribed by a doctor for specific medical conditions. Steroids can cause many health problems, especially in children. Hair loss, stunted growth, sterility, heart disease, liver damage, and cancer are just some of the unwanted side effects that steroids can produce. Personality changes, including sudden flare-ups of aggressive " 'roid rage," can also occur.

Why would anyone want to experiment with such potentially dangerous drugs?

People don't take steroids for the same reasons they take other drugs. They aren't trying to feel "high" or to relax or to escape from problems. People take anabolic steroids because these drugs stimulate growth—especially muscle growth. Steroid users want to be stronger, or to look stronger. Don Leggett, of the Food and Drug Administration, says, "Bulging muscles are in. Guys want to look good at the beach. High-school kids think steroids may enhance their ability to get an athletic scholarship, play pro sports or win the girl of their heart."

Michigan teenager Michael Keys was one of these young people who thought steroids held the answer to his problems. As a child, he was small for his age, and classmates often picked on him. He thought of himself as a weakling. When he was thirteen, he started lifting weights. Three years later he was a muscular 165 pounds, but he still wasn't satisfied. Other boys he knew were using steroids and bulking up even faster. Michael began taking the drugs, too, and within a year he had gained nearly thirty more pounds of muscle. But the popularity he had hoped for did not come along. He couldn't seem to keep a girlfriend, and his family and friends noticed that he seemed to be getting more aggressive and irritable. "He took everything the wrong way," says his brother Philip. "You'd say one word, and he'd get upset and walk away." He had trouble concentrating on his schoolwork, too, and his grades began to go down. Michael told his worried parents that he was getting off steroids. But one December day, when he was seventeen, he put a rifle to his head and pulled the trigger.

When Canadian sprinter Ben Johnson was stripped of his Olympic medal, he lost his claim to a world record, his reputation, and millions of dollars he might have received for endorsements. Many people hoped that this spectacular example of what can happen when you take steroids would help deter young people from using the drugs. But many experts are worried that the result has been just the opposite. Bob Goldman, chief physician and chairman of the drug testing committee of the International Federation of Body Builders, noted, "Since the Ben Johnson episode, kids are coming into gyms asking for steroids because they want to run faster."

Many experts believe that so many young people are taking steroids because they either aren't aware of the dangers or don't believe reports they've heard. Until recently, many athletes were even encouraged to take steroids by parents and school coaches who weren't aware of the possible dangers.

In the chapters that follow, you will learn about steroids (commonly called "roids," "juice," and "gas"): an explanation of what they are, the reasons people use them, their history, and their positive and negative effects. We'll also discuss other drugs that are used to help athletes perform better in sports, and we'll explore both sides of the debate over whether using drugs to enhance performance is fair or not.

References

Articles

Altman, Lawrence. "New 'Breakfast of Champions': A Recipe for Victory or Disaster?" *The New York Times,* November 20, 1988, pp. 1, 34.

Brody, Jane E. "Spreading Use of Steroids by Young Athletes Alarms Sports Medicine Specialists." *The New York Times,* February 18, 1988, p. B8.

Brower, Montgomery, and Carol Azizian. "Steroids Built Mike Keys Up; Then They Tore Him Down." *People,* March 20, 1989, pp. 107–108.

Charlier, Marj. "Among Teen-Agers, Abuse of Steroids May Be Bigger Issue Than Cocaine Use." *Wall Street Journal,* October 4, 1988, p. A20.

Chelminski, Rudolph. "The Shocking Stain on International Athletics." *Reader's Digest,* August 1988, pp. 131–135.

Cowart, Virginia S. "Athletes and Steroids: The Bad Bargain." *Saturday Evening Post,* April 1987, pp. 56–59.

Fackelmann, K. A. "Male Teenagers at Risk of Steroid Abuse." *Science News,* February 17, 1988, p. 25.

Maugh, Thomas H., II, "Steroid Abuse: Turning Winners Into Losers." *World Book Health and Medical Annual 1990,* Chicago: World Book, 1989, pp. 42–55.

Rowan, Carl, and David Mazie. "The Mounting Menace of Steroids." *Reader's Digest,* February 1988, pp. 133–137.

Slothower, Jodie. "Mean Mental Muscles: The Psychological Price of Steroids." *Health,* January 1988, p. 20.

Toufexis, Anastasia. "Shortcut to the Rambo Look." *Time,* January 30, 1989, p. 78.

Books

Goldman, Bob. *Death in the Locker Room.* South Bend, Ind.: Icarus Press, 1984.

Mohun, Janet. *Drugs, Steroids, and Sports.* New York: Franklin Watts, 1988.

Nuwer, Hank. *Steroids.* New York: Franklin Watts, 1990.

Wadler, Gary I., and Brian Hainline. *Drugs and the Athlete.* Philadelphia: F. A. Davis, 1989.

2

What Are Steroids?

The steroids that have been in the news lately are man-made forms, called *anabolic steroids*. They are only part of a far larger group of chemicals. There are hundreds of naturally occurring steroids, as well as thousands of synthetic ones.

The natural steroids are an important class of compounds, produced by virtually all living things—animals, plants, and even bacteria. All the different kinds of steroids have similar chemical structures. They all share the same basic steroid ring system: a chain of seventeen carbon atoms, looped around and linked together by chemical bonds to form four fused rings. Various atoms and groups are attached to the rings. The differences in these attached groups give rise to the huge variety of the natural and synthetic steroids and determine the striking differences in their effects on living creatures.

Digitalis, a plant steroid, was first used in the eighteenth century as a medication for heart conditions, and it is still used today. Many plants produce steroids that are fatal in large doses; their function is to keep insects away. Some toads excrete poisonous steroids to keep predators away. Steroid hormones, produced in far smaller amounts, play equally vital roles. They act as chemical messengers, helping to control and coordinate body functions.

Birth-control pills are the most widely used steroid drugs. Oral contraceptives were first introduced in the early 1960s; today, most birth-control pills are combinations of synthetic steroids produced from the plant steroid diosgenin, which comes from wild yams.

The Body Steroids

Two main types of steroids are produced in the human body. The adrenal steroids are produced by the adrenal glands, two walnut-sized organs perched on top of the kidneys. These steroids control many body processes and are especially important in the responses to stress. The other major type is the sex hormones: estrogen, progesterone, and testosterone. Estrogen and progesterone are female sex hormones, produced in the ovaries (the female sex organs). Testosterone is an androgen (a male sex hormone). As might be expected, it is produced in the testes, the male sex organs; but, somewhat unexpectedly, testosterone is also produced in the adrenal glands—and in the ovaries of females!

The production of all steroids is thought to start out from a chemical called squalene, which is a very common body chemical. Most steroids are formed in plants and animals through similar reactions involving acetic acid (the acid that gives the tang to vinegar) and enzymes. These transform squalene into a steroid called lanosterol in animals, and into cycloartenol in plants; both of these intermediate products can be converted further into cholesterol.

Cholesterol is the most common steroid in the body. All the body steroids, both adrenal and sex hormones, come from cholesterol. Maybe you've heard that cholesterol is "bad." News features and TV commercials warn against cholesterol in the diet and imply that it is harmful to health. Perhaps you know someone who has had to cut down on eggs, red meat, and fatty foods because blood tests have shown that his or her "cholesterol level" is too high. Doctors warn that in some people cholesterol can contribute to the buildup of fatty deposits in the arteries, which can lead to heart disease. Actually, though, the body needs a certain amount of cholesterol—without it, we would die. Cholesterol is an important part of the cell membranes that surround most of the trillions of body cells. Cholesterol is also changed into bile acids (which are produced by the liver and help the body to digest fats) and steroid hormones in animals, and into steroidlike alkaloids in plants.

The steroid secretions from the adrenal glands, ovaries, and testes are controlled by a part of the brain called the hypothalamus. It works by regulating the amounts of hormones released from the pituitary gland. These pituitary hormones, gonadotropins and adrenocorticotropic hormone (ACTH), are proteins. They cause the steroid-producing centers (adrenal glands, ovaries, and testes) to produce steroids, which then influence many different organs of the body.

Adrenal Steroids

Adrenal steroids are also called cortical steroids, or adrenocorticoid hormones, because they are formed in the cortex—the outer layer of the two adrenal glands.

The adrenal steroids include cortisol, corticosterone, and cortisone, which help to regulate protein and carbohydrate metabolism. Another adrenal steroid, aldosterone, is involved in maintaining the mineral and water balance in the body. Adrenal steroids like cortisone, prednisone, and hydrocortisone reduce inflammation and are used in medicine to treat arthritis, allergies, asthma, certain types of cancer, and adrenal deficiencies, as well as inflammation due to injury. In experimental studies, prednisone has been found to delay the effects of a type of muscular dystrophy in children. Medical researchers have recently discovered that prompt injections of another anti-inflammatory steroid, methylprednisolone, after a spinal cord injury can help to prevent paralysis.

Adrenal steroids are a key part of the body's defenses against stress. After an injury, they help to provide the body with the energy needed to defend itself from damage and also to keep the blood pressure at the necessary level. These are not the steroids that athletes abuse to build up muscles. In fact, adrenal steroids may even reduce muscle tissue.

Sex Hormones

The sex steroids help to stimulate and maintain the sex organs and the secondary sex characteristics that distinguish male from female; they also have some more general effects on the body.

Estrogens and progesterone are female sex hormones that are produced by the ovaries in females. These steroids are responsible for the female characteristics, including a high-pitched voice, smooth skin, a broad hip structure, and the typical female pattern of fat distribution that gives shape to the breasts and produces rounded curves. Birth-control pills are synthetic forms of progesterone and estrogens. The male sex organs also produce estrogens, but in much smaller quantities.

Testosterone and other androgens are the male steroid hormones, produced by the male testes and the adrenal cortex. Testosterone is responsible for male secondary sex characteristics such as a beard, deep voice, and a slim-hipped, muscular body build. Female sex organs also produce androgens, but in much smaller quantities. (It is the proportion of male and female sex hormones circulating in the blood that determines whether a person will develop a male or female appearance.)

In addition to their androgenic (masculinizing) effects, the male sex hormones also have more general, anabolic effects. "Anabolic" refers to the chemical reactions in the body that result in a building up of tissues and structures, in contrast to "catabolic" reactions that break down body tissues. Androgens stimulate appetite and promote growth, the building of muscle proteins, and the formation of red blood cells.

Anabolic Steroids

Anabolic steroids are synthetic variations of the male sex hormone, testosterone. These steroids are designed to emphasize the anabolic effects, building muscle without masculinizing the user as much as testosterone does.

Anabolic steroids were used after World War II to treat some types of breast cancer in women by reducing the overall proportion of estrogens. (The female sex hormones not only stimulate normal breast development but also promote the growth of tumors formed from breast tissue.) They have also been used to treat two rare types of anemia, angioedema (a hereditary allergic reaction to various foods), insect bites, severe burns, muscle-wasting diseases, some endocrine gland disorders, certain types of osteoporosis, and sometimes have been given to geriatric patients after operations to help repair tissue and encourage muscle growth. They are being used experimentally to help prevent the wasting effects of AIDS. However, the FDA says that better drugs, or alternative drugs, have been developed to treat the ailments for which anabolic steroids have been used.

Anabolic steroids do not have anti-inflammatory properties like the adrenal steroids, but many athletes who take them rationalize by saying they are using them to treat and prevent injury. The main reason that young people take steroids, though, is for their muscle-building effects. Typically, they start with oral steroids such as Dianabol, Anadro, Primobolan, and Anavar. The idea of injecting drugs may seem a bit scary, while taking pills seems comfortingly familiar in today's world. After a while, though, many steroid users progress to injected drugs such as Depo-Testosterone and Deca-Durabolin, which can give a more powerful effect. The first injection is usually given by a steroid-using friend, an athletic coach, or a drug dealer, but soon users learn to do it themselves. Typically, the drugs are taken in cycles of four to eighteen weeks, and then stopped. But Dr. William Taylor of the American College of Sports Medicine says that after just one cycle, about 40 percent of steroid users become abusers.

In the following chapters we'll take a closer look at the effects of anabolic steroids on the body and the ways in which they are being used—and abused.

References

Articles

Brody, Jane. "Spreading Use of Steroids by Young Athletes Alarms Sports Medicine Specialists." *The New York Times,* February 18, 1988, p. B8.

Cowart, Virginia S. "Athletes and Steroids: The Bad Bargain." *Saturday Evening Post,* April 1987, pp. 56–59.

Hecht, Annabel. "Anabolic Steroids: Pumping Trouble." *FDA Consumer,* September 1984, pp. 12–15.

Jackson, Lynn M. "Steroids Are as Addictive as Any Other Drug." *Courier-News* (Bridgewater, N.J.), May 3, 1991, p. B6.

Maugh, Thomas H., II. "Steroid Abuse: Turning Winners Into Losers." *World Book Health and Medical Annual 1990,* Chicago: World Book, 1989, pp. 42–55.

Miller, Roger W. "Athletes and Steroids: Playing a Deadly Game." *FDA Consumer,* November 1987, pp. 17–21.

Mirkin, Gabe. "Hormonal Helpers." *Health,* March 1984, pp. 6, 46.

Stehlin, Dori. "For Athletes and Dealers, Black Market Steroids Are Risky Business." *FDA Consumer,* September 1987, pp. 24–25.

Books

Goldman, Bob. *Death in the Locker Room.* South Bend, Ind.: Icarus Press, 1984.

Wadler, Gary I., and Brian Hainline. *Drugs and the Athlete.* Philadelphia: F. A. Davis, 1989.

Witzmann, Rupert F. *Steroids: Keys to Life.* New York: Van Nostrand-Reinhold, 1981.

3

Anabolic Steroids: Who Uses Them and Why?

Anabolic steroids were developed in the 1930s to treat anemia, malnutrition, and skeletal problems. It wasn't long, though, before these new synthetic drugs were being abused. In Germany, Hitler sponsored a research and development project, hoping to use anabolic steroids to build an army of supermen. During World War II, the Nazi troops were given the drugs to make them more aggressive in battle. After the war ended, anabolic steroids were put to a more humanitarian use, helping to build up the wasted bodies of concentration camp survivors.

Steroids in Sports

In the 1950s, Soviet and East European Olympic athletes began using steroids to boost their power in Olympic and international competitions. During this time they dominated the world in strength events.

A Russian physician told Dr. John Ziegler, the team physician of the United States weight-lifting team at the 1954 world championships, that many of the Russian competitors were taking testosterone to enhance their performance. Dr. Ziegler was impressed by what he saw, and in 1959 he began conducting his own steroid experiments.

The Russian men and women who took the hormones took such large doses that many looked overly masculine. The women looked so much like men that chromosome tests were required to verify that they were really women. Dr. Ziegler hoped to develop a synthetic version of testosterone that would have much less masculinizing effects.

American Olympic weight lifters began using these anabolic steroids in the 1960s. Dr. Ziegler later regretted introducing steroids to American sports. "I wish I had never heard the word 'steroid,' " he said. "These kids don't realize the terrible price they are going to pay." Dr. Ziegler hadn't realized how the drugs would be abused. Many of the athletes who used the drug had obsessive personalities. They were

so pleased with their gains in weight and strength that they did not stick to the recommended doses. They figured if a little is good, more would be better—so they took as much as twenty times the prescribed amounts. Dr. Ziegler stopped his tests of anabolic steroids when he found that some of the athletes taking them had developed liver problems.

It was too late. Steroid use in sports was already spreading. Other athletes heard about the drugs and were eager to apply their benefits to their own sports. Shot putters, discus and hammer throwers were soon using steroids. Then football players, sprinters, and swimmers, as well, realized steroids could be useful in their training. From 6 to 8 percent of professional football players test positive for steroids each year, but sports drug experts believe that is only the tip of the iceberg. In fact, *Sports Illustrated* has declared that up to 80 percent of NFL football linemen and half of the linebackers have used steroids. According to other estimates, up to half of all world-class athletes have used illegal drugs to enhance their performance.

As more and more athletes used and praised steroids, amateur athletes in college and high school began using them, too. Some reports indicate that up to 20 percent of high school athletes use steroids. One study found that 38 percent of high school football players knew where to get these drugs.

Bodybuilders had long been using steroids to help pump up their muscles. But for a long time the overly developed muscles of bodybuilders —particularly in women—were not considered attractive. After the enormously popular movie *Pumping Iron,* bulging muscles became more fashionable, and average people began to work out to try and attain the "ideal" physique. Steroids became a valuable tool in helping to develop muscles and strength in gymnasiums across the country. In a survey conducted by Dr. William N. Taylor, a member of the U.S. Olympic Drug Control program, 90 percent of the members of some health clubs had used steroids. Dr. Taylor declared that steroid use in our country has reached "epidemic proportions." "It's not a sports problem anymore," he said. "It's a social problem."

Today's Steroid Epidemic

The 1988 Olympic games helped make the world aware of the real problem of steroids in today's sports. Experts had estimated that as many as one million Americans were using steroids. That figure was awesome enough for most health officials, but the problem is probably bigger than even the experts had thought. In December 1988, the results of a study conducted by researchers at Pennsylvania State University suggested that there may be as many as 500,000 teenage steroid users!

According to the study, more than one in fifteen high school senior males had used anabolic steroids, and two-thirds of them had started before they were sixteen! The researchers believe that the numbers of

The majority of high school football players, like these, develop their natural abilities, but numbers of steroid users are growing ominously at all levels of sports.

high school steroid users are probably even higher than the students admitted.

The Penn State researchers discovered several other surprising statistics, as well. Nearly 40 percent of the steroid users "stacked" steroids, which means they used more than one type of steroid at a time. Nearly 40 percent of the users injected steroids as well as taking them in pill form. Health officials are concerned about this fact because many drug users reuse needles, and in addition to possible infections, AIDS transmission through shared needles is a very real possibility.

One-third of high school steroid users do not participate in sports. They use the drugs solely to enhance their appearance. They are seeking a shortcut to looking like a muscle-bound superman. One quarter of the students polled said they were convinced of the benefits of using steroids and had no intention of stopping their use.

The study also found that there seemed to be no boundaries to steroid use. Rich, poor, urban, and rural schools all seemed to be affected. In fact, steroid use has spread throughout all society. Even some police officers have been found to be using steroids to make themselves seem more threatening to criminals. A Florida police chief commented, "There's a great potential for an officer abusing steroids to physically mistreat people."

Why Do People Use Steroids?

There are many reasons why people use steroids. But the two main ones are to excel in athletic competition and to look more like one's ideal of a perfect body.

Athletes turn to steroids because they feel the need to "win at any cost." Olympic doctor John Lombardo found that 80 percent of the Olympic athletes he polled from all countries said they would use steroids if it increased their chances of winning a gold medal.

Sports are much more than just friendly competition. In high school, excelling in sports could help a student to get into a good college. It can help a teenager find self-esteem and feelings of pride and identity. Many parents and athletic coaches consider athletics as important as classroom learning, if not more important. Young athletes can feel an enormous amount of pressure to do well.

Doing well in college sports can be a ticket into professional sports, as well as the maintenance of a sense of accomplishment and pride. Professional sports winners gain much more than pride. They gain fame and are idolized by millions. They can earn tremendous salaries for playing their sport, and many stars continue to reap the benefits long after they retire with numerous endorsements that bank on their star reputation.

For all of these reasons and many others, many athletes feel tremendous pressure to do well. For some, this desire to succeed will force them to win at any cost. Some turn to drugs that they think will help them compete and give them a better chance at winning. For some, the desire to win is the most important thing in their lives. One hundred runners were asked if they would take a drug that would make them Olympic champions, even if they knew they would die from the effects of the drug within a year. Half of the athletes said they would gladly take the drug!

Drugs are intended to be taken by those who have something wrong with them. The drugs may have negative side effects, but their benefits in curing ailments outweigh the risks. When healthy people take drugs to help them do better at something, it is harder to justify the possible risks. Moreover, the chances of harmful effects are greatly increased. Those who take drugs to improve their performance often take them for a long time and in high doses, which makes problems more likely.

Drug users in sports endanger more than their health. They risk losing everything if they are caught. Rules have become stricter in most competitive sports, and drug users can be suspended from participating. In addition, they risk losing the respect of the fans who once admired them.

These risks and penalties are balanced by some strong motivations. Mottos like "May the best person win" and "It's not whether you win or lose but how you play the game" express the ideals of sportsmanship and fair competition, but all too often they become empty words. In today's world, the person who comes in first is remembered and hailed as a hero; the "also rans" are often quickly forgotten, no matter how hard they tried. For many competitors the stakes are too high. There is so much pressure to perform—to be *the best*. And there is always a new crop of competitors, waiting for their own big chance and ready to take the place of anyone who falters.

Many athletes feel they have to use steroids just to survive. Other competitors are using drugs, so if they don't, they won't have a chance against the drug users. Steve Korte, center for the New Orleans Saints, once declared, "Look, I don't want to use steroids, but I'm a center, and any time I go against a big nose guard, like I do every week, there's a good chance he's taking them. So if I don't take them, I'm at a disadvantage." He said that when he wasn't taking steroids, he felt "sore and weak and beat up" the day after a game but with steroids he felt as though he was "ready to go again."

The other main reason for steroid use is to build self-esteem by "improving" one's appearance. Adolescence can be a trying time for teenage boys, who are beginning to feel like men but may still have a "child's" body. Early in childhood we learn that the ideal man has bulging muscles. Rambo, Arnold Schwarzenegger, Hulk Hogan, and other heroes are pumped up, almost larger than life. Even in cartoons the heroes are abnormally muscle-bound. Football stars and Olympic athletes are all extremely muscular. "Little boys are always looking up to the stronger, powerful men, you know, like muscles," says Tom, a New Jersey teenager who started taking steroids when he was fifteen because he felt he was too "skinny." Many teenage boys like Tom are turning to steroids to help speed up the process of looking more like a "man." Those who combine steroids with weight training get results that encourage them to continue to use the drugs.

Bodybuilder Arnold Schwarzenegger, now chairman of the President's Council on Physical Fitness, is a role model for many young people.

Another reason people turn to drugs so quickly for answers to problems is that our society is very drug oriented. "Legal drugs" are a part of nearly everyone's lives. We use drugs to stop pain, to stay awake, to go to sleep, to give us energy, to lose weight, to feel good, as well as to make us well when we're ill. With our modern technology, most people expect these "scientific aids" to work efficiently and fast.

Society also has a very lenient attitude toward changing one's appearance to look more like the "ideal" man or woman. Cosmetic surgery, orthodontic braces, Nautilus machines, and fad diets all reaffirm the view that there is a "right" way to look. Bigger, taller, leaner, and more fit are seen as ideals that everyone should strive for. Kids and adults may regard steroids as just another method to use in achieving that goal.

Are Steroids Addictive?

The young man who arrived at a hospital emergency room in Ann Arbor, Michigan, one night in 1987 seemed to be in perfect health. His strong, muscular build reflected the long hours he had put in at the gym, and he regularly bench-pressed twice his own weight. He didn't drink or smoke, thought mind-altering drugs were strictly for chumps, and didn't even eat junk food. But for months he had been plagued by wild mood swings and outbursts of rage. His wife had left him, and now he was fighting suicidal impulses to steer his car into the oncoming traffic. As the doctors questioned him, they discovered that he had been taking anabolic steroids as an aid to his weight training. He had been trying to quit for the past nine months, but each time he cut down the dose, he suffered from headaches, fatigue, and depression.

"It was the classic syndrome you see in anybody suffering from chemical dependency," comments Kirk Brower, the University of Michigan psychiatrist who counseled the man. "But that had never been reported in someone taking steroids."

Most steroid users start out believing that they will use steroids for a short time only to help them get into better shape or to achieve the look they want. But when steroids and training stop, muscles fade away. Steroids are very hard to give up when people's whole self-image (the way they think about themselves) depends on the way they look or the way they perform. Some recent studies suggest that once people have begun taking steroids, whatever their original motivation, they may have difficulty stopping when they want to. Users may become "hooked" on the drugs.

Charles Yesalis of Pennsylvania State University, who coauthored the 1988 survey of high school seniors, believes that steroid users are prompted to continue by a psychological dependence rather than an actual physical addiction. This dependence results from the user's satisfaction with the results the drug produces in the body and his or her "ability to perform and train at high intensity," he says. Dr. William Taylor at Washington State University notes, " Very few steroid users want to stop. When they do stop, muscle mass decreases, body fat goes up, energy and sex drive diminish. They feel depressed and miss the powerful, hyped-up feeling the drug gives them."

Some experts, like Dr. Robert Voy, former director of sports medicine and science for the U.S. Olympic Committee, say that the effects of stopping steroid use are not just psychological but true withdrawal symptoms, typical of an actual physical addiction.

Yale University School of Medicine psychiatrists Kenneth Kashkin and Herbert Kleber found evidence to support this view. Their observations of steroid users revealed that those who stopped taking the drugs experienced a craving for steroids and typical withdrawal symptoms when the drug levels in their bodies dropped suddenly. High levels of anabolic steroids in the body produces a sense of well being, the Yale researchers say; users can become happy, talkative, and euphoric. At first, withdrawal produces symptoms similar to withdrawal from alcohol: anxiety, irritability, sleep difficulties, muscle aches, and hot and cold flashes. Later the former user may become depressed, even suicidal—much like the pattern observed in cocaine addicts trying to quit.

Drs. Kashkin and Kleber compare these effects to those of fluctuations in the level of natural hormones: the depressed mood of some women when the levels of female hormones drop just before menstruation or after childbirth, for example. They claim that anabolic steroids can change people's moods and can produce a "previously unrecognized drug addiction," with all the typical characteristics of other drug addictions:

—use of the drug continues longer than the user intended;

—attempts to stop are unsuccessful;

—drug use becomes a focus of the user's life, and a great deal of time is spent obtaining, using, or recovering from the drug;

—stopping the drug brings on withdrawal symptoms;

—these withdrawal symptoms can be relieved by another dose of the drug or a substitute for it.

Psychiatrist Kirk Brower also is firmly convinced that anabolic steroids can be addictive. He and his colleagues distributed anonymous questionnaires to bodybuilders at local gyms; more than half of the forty-five who replied reported three or more symptoms of chemical dependency. Nearly all reported at least one symptom—most commonly a deep fatigue or depression experienced when they tried to stop the drugs.

Drug experts are still debating whether anabolic steroids should be considered addictive drugs. What is certain is that they can have powerful effects on the body. But surprisingly, there is a great deal of disagreement on whether they have the bodybuilding effects that users claim they do.

References

Articles

Brody, Jane E. "Spreading Use of Steroids by Young Athletes Alarms Sports Medicine Specialists." *The New York Times,* February 18, 1988, p. B8.

Brower, Montgomery, and Carol Azizian. "Steroids Built Mike Keys Up; Then They Tore Him Down." *People,* March 20, 1989, pp. 107–108.

Brubaker, Bill. "Players Close Eyes to Steroids' Risks." *Washington Post,* February 1, 1987, pp. C1, C13.

Charlier, Marj. "Among Teen-Agers, Abuse of Steroids May Be Bigger Issue Than Cocaine Use." *Wall Street Journal,* October 4, 1988, p. A20.

Chelminski, Rudolph. "The Shocking Stain on International Athletics." *Reader's Digest,* August 1988, pp. 131–135.

Couzens, Gerald Secor. "Steroid Users Learn the Price of Success." *Star-Ledger* (Newark, N.J.), March 5, 1989, p. 11.

Cowart, Virginia S. "Athletes and Steroids: The Bad Bargain." *Saturday Evening Post,* April 1987, pp. 56–59.

Fackelmann, K. A. "Male Teenagers at Risk of Steroid Abuse," *Science News,* February 17, 1988, p. 25.

Franklin, Deborah. "Stuck on Steroids?" *In Health,* May/June, 1990, pp. 22–23.

Hecht, Annabel. "Anabolic Steroids: Pumping Trouble." *FDA Consumer,* September 1984, pp. 12–15.

Jackson, Lynn M. "Steroids Are as Addictive as Any Other Drug." *Courier-News* (Bridgewater, N.J.), May 3, 1991, p. B6.

Johnson, Karl. "Giants MD Lines Up on Side of Steroid Foes." *Star-Ledger* (Newark, N.J.), March 12, 1989, p. 15.

Marshall, Eliot. "The Drug of Champions." *Science,* October 14, 1988, pp. 183–184.

Maugh, Thomas H., II. "Steroid Abuse: Turning Winners Into Losers." *World Book Health and Medical Annual 1990,* Chicago: World Book 1989, pp. 42–55.

McDaniel, Jay. "Steroids in the Schools," *Star-Ledger* (Newark, N.J.), March 15, 1989, p. 16.

Miller, Roger W. "Athletes and Steroids: Playing a Deadly Game." *FDA Consumer,* November 1987, pp. 17–21.

Rowan, Carl, and David Mazie. "The Mounting Menace of Steroids." *Reader's Digest,* February 1988, pp. 133–137.

Yesalis, Charles. "Steroid Use Is Not Just an Adult Problem." *The New York Times,* December 4, 1988, p. 12.

Books

Mohun, Janet. *Drugs, Steroids, and Sports.* New York: Franklin Watts, 1988.

Nuwer, Hand. *Steroids.* New York: Franklin Watts, 1990.

4

Do Steroids Work?

Until a few years ago, the general opinion in the medical field was that steroids didn't really help athletes gain muscle tissue. The athletes only thought that steroids would help them train, and so they worked harder. It was this focused attitude and the physical stimulation of training that produced the bodybuilding effects, rather than any real changes produced by the drugs themselves. Doctors call this kind of result a placebo effect.

Of course, the steroid-using athletes thought this argument was silly. Their friends who used steroids got bigger muscles. When they used steroids, their muscles got bigger too. They began to think that the doctors didn't really know what they were talking about when it came to steroids.

Yet the medical experts could point to numerous carefully controlled studies in which some volunteers took anabolic steroids while others received placebos—sugar pills or other substances known to have no medical effect on their own. The results were confusingly inconsistent. Herbert A. Haupt, a St. Louis orthopedic surgeon, and his associate, G. D. Rovere, looked at twenty-four studies on steroids. Fourteen of the studies showed that steroids do enhance athletic performance, but the findings of the other ten indicated that they do not. Dr. Haupt found that the main difference between the two batches of studies is that the fourteen that supported a correlation between steroid use and improved athletic performance involved athletes who trained rigorously.

Another problem with the scientific tests was that they involved small doses of the drugs. But in real life, athletes often take ten to one hundred times the therapeutic doses. These doses may have a different effect than small doses do. Athletes also tend to mix drugs, "stacking" several different steroids at once, which can further confuse the results. Moreover, the differences being measured may be very small and might easily be missed unless very large numbers of subjects are included in the tests.

The Current View

As the evidence continued to accumulate, the medical community gradually changed its opinion on steroids. Today, most doctors believe that steroids can build muscles under certain conditions. Just taking the drug will not guarantee the development of larger muscles. The use of steroids can increase muscle mass and strength only when the users are involved in a continuing program of high-intensity exercise and eat a high-protein diet. This is the current view of the American Medical Association, and also of the American College of Sports

THE WIZARD OF ID   Brant parker and Johnny hart

34

Medicine; but they caution that steroid use can also be damaging to health.

Typical of the recent studies is a 1989 report by the Cleveland Clinic Foundation that bodybuilders who used steroids gained an average of nearly nine pounds of lean muscle in ten weeks. The weight of a control group of bodybuilders, who trained just as hard but did not use drugs, remained constant.

Steroids thus seem to speed up the natural process of building muscles that happens with vigorous exercise. They are believed to produce this effect by blocking the breakdown of muscle tissue, which occurs in straining exercise. Instead, the chemical balance of the muscles is altered, and muscle tissue growth increases. In addition, steroids also improve the use of the proteins in foods, using their amino acids as the building blocks for new muscle tissue.

In 1988, a study in the *British Medical Journal* reported that anabolic steroids can increase the size of a type of muscle fiber even without any training. Stanozolol, the steroid Ben Johnson tested positive for, was found to increase the size of endurance muscle (Type I muscle tissue) in the abdominal muscles of patients who were scheduled for surgery. This type of muscle tends to increase in size after doing exercise over a long period of time—but the subjects of the British study did no additional exercise. The steroid did not increase the size of Type II muscle, which enlarges after strength-building exercises. Researchers are only beginning to explore what these findings might mean.

The medical community has gradually changed its view on the bodybuilding effects of anabolic steroids, but the opinion on the potential dangers of these powerful drugs has not changed. These unwanted (and sometimes fatal) side effects will be discussed in the next chapter.

References

Articles

Altman, Lawrence. "New 'Breakfast of Champions': A Recipe for Victory or Disaster?" *The New York Times,* November 20, 1988, pp. 1, 34.

Franklin, Deborah. "Stuck on Steroids?" *In Health,* May/June, 1990, pp. 22–23.

Marshall, Eliot. "The Drug of Champions." *Science,* October 14, 1988, pp. 183–184.

Maugh, Thomas H., II. "Steroid Abuse: Turning Winners Into Losers," *World Book Health and Medical Annual 1990,* Chicago: World Book, 1989, pp. 42–55.

Miller, Roger W. "Athletes and Steroids: Playing a Deadly Game." *FDA Consumer,* November 1987, pp. 17–21.

Taylor, William N. "Super Athletes Made to Order." *Psychology Today,* May 1985, pp. 63–66.

Books

Nuwer, Hank. *Steroids.* New York: Franklin Watts, 1990.

Wadler, Gary I., and Brian Hainline. *Drugs and the Athlete.* Philadelphia: F. A. Davis, 1989.

5

Dangers of Steroids

Steroids probably do help some people to increase their strength and muscle size. The ethical aspect—does steroid use give the users an unfair advantage?—will be discussed later. First, let's examine the main reason health officials are concerned with steroids—that they can be dangerous to one's health.

Most steroid users have heard that steroids can be harmful. Why don't they listen? Steroid researcher Jim Wright points out that the dangers of the drugs don't seem to have much personal reality to the average teenage user. "Kids can't really conceive of their own mortality," he says. "You always believe at that age that you're going to be the one that survives." Nick, a nineteen-year-old bodybuilder from New Jersey, has that kind of attitude. "I know the dangers, but I try not to think about it that much," he comments. "I try to block it out. I enjoy what they do, and that kind of overrides the negative. The negative is down the road; the positive is happening now."

Another factor that makes the dangers of steroid use seem unreal is that the most serious side effects are rather rare. "Nobody has dropped dead," comments Bruce Wilhelm, a former Olympic weight lifter. Actually, there have been some highly publicized deaths of athletes who were taking steroids. West German athlete Birgit Dressel, for example, had hoped to win a gold medal in the 1988 Olympics. But she died suddenly in 1987 after taking a cocktail of two anabolic steroids. Doctors believed her death was due to the massive breakdown of her immune system caused by steroid abuse. But the athlete had also been taking various combination of numerous other drugs in an attempt to aid her training. In this case, as in others, doctors could not pinpoint the steroids as the definite cause of death. For the average steroid user, such cases seem hyped and very remote from real experience. The users have friends who have also been using steroids and seem to be strong and healthy. They don't believe the warnings of medical experts—especially since doctors were saying just a few years ago that steroids don't work and now they concede that steroids can help build muscle, after all. "Anything organized medicine says right now will probably be ignored," says Dr. James Garrick, a sports medicine specialist in San Francisco.

That is unfortunate; evidence is accumulating that steroid abuse can be dangerous.

"Steroids may not kill you in a dramatic fashion like a cocaine overdose, but if an athlete uses steroids, liver damage and premature coronary artery disease caused by the body's increased cholesterol and elevated blood pressure will most likely contribute to an athlete's eventual demise," says Dr. Bob Goldman. A noted authority on anabolic steroids, he is the author of *Death in the Locker Room*, a book that opens dramatically with the story of a twenty-three-year-old bodybuilder friend who died from liver and kidney failure while taking steroids.

The fact is that there are dozens of proven side effects of anabolic steroids given in therapeutic doses, ranging from acne to liver abnormalities and an increased risk of heart disease. But no testing has even been done involving the huge quantities of steroid drugs that users take. (Even if athletes were to volunteer to be tested scientifically, these tests would never pass an ethics review committee—which is required for all drug testing on humans.) If small doses can produce damage, the effects of larger doses are probably even worse.

The synthesis of anabolic steroids is designed to minimize or eliminate the masculinizing effects of the natural androgens. But experts say that none of the anabolic steroids available are completely free of masculinizing effects. Therefore, when steroid users take the drug, their bodies receive the impression that there is an increased amount of testosterone circulating in the blood. An adult man's body produces 2.5 to 10 mg of testosterone each day. But steroid users take 10 to 100 times that amount of steroids. Testosterone affects the development of bone, muscle, skin, and hair, in addition to producing emotional changes. The increased amount of the male hormone supplied by the synthetic steroids can confuse the coordination of the body reactions, and the normal testosterone functions can be thrown off.

Effects on Males

At first, the use of anabolic steroids may increase the sex drive, but interest in sex soon drops off. When a male takes steroids, his body slows down its own production of testosterone and may stop making this vital hormone altogether. But remember that everyone has both male and female hormones; it is the ratio that determines the development of secondary sex characteristics like a beard or breasts. When high levels of anabolic steroids result in a shutdown of the production of the real male hormone, testosterone, the estrogen levels in the body remain the same; so the result may be a feminizing effect! Male steroid users sometimes develop larger breasts and shrunken testicles; their sperm production drops, and they may suffer temporary impotence. Severe acne is another annoying side effect of the unbalanced hormone levels. These symptoms often disappear when steroid use is stopped, but the hormone levels may take a long time to return to normal. (There is some concern about possible long-term effects in male users.)

Effects on Females

In females, anabolic steroids greatly increase the proportion of androgenlike hormones circulating in the body. As a result, the female user's voice may become deeper, her breasts get smaller, facial hair may develop, and male pattern baldness (which usually affects only men) may cause a loss of hair. In addition, the clitoris may become enlarged, the uterus may become atrophied, and menstrual irregularities may occur. Acne is a common side effect for female users, as well as males. The masculinizing changes may appear after only a few months of steroid use, and—unlike the side effects in male users—the changes that occur may be permanent.

Effects on Adolescents

Steroids are particularly dangerous for adolescents because their bodies are still developing. Steroids can quicken adulthood in adolescent males who have not yet reached puberty. (Doctors sometimes use anabolic steroids for boys who are late in reaching puberty.) One side effect of reaching adulthood sooner may be premature baldness. More importantly, steroids may stunt an adolescent's growth. Steroids can cause the growth plates in the long bones in the arms and legs to close permanently, preventing any further growth. The person thus may end up shorter than he or she would have been without steroids. The young steroid user does become more muscular, but the weight gain may turn out to be a long-term trap. Muscle tissue needs regular exercise to be maintained; otherwise, it tends to waste away. Someone who has used steroids as an adolescent may become less active in later life and find that high-calorie eating habits are producing deposits of flabby fat. It is ironic that scrawny teenage boys take steroids to become big, strong hunks but may wind up short and fat as adults.

Even at the height of the muscle buildup, the results of steroid use may not bring the social rewards that scrawny teenagers dream of. One teenager who had started taking steroids because girls called him a "wimp" found that only his male friends really admired his newly developed muscles. "I didn't do too well with the girls when I was on," he commented. "Maybe I didn't care, I was too into myself. I was really big; maybe I did scare 'em off."

Cardiovascular Effects

Steroid use can have many other, even more serious consequences. In one study of bodybuilders, for example, all those who took steroids showed a dramatic increase in body cholesterol after six weeks. "Bad cholesterol"—low-density lipoprotein cholesterol (the form that contributes to deposits in the arteries)—levels rose, and "good cholesterol"—high-density lipoprotein cholesterol (the form in which cholesterol is removed from the arteries)—dropped significantly. Dr. Herbert K. Naito of the Cleveland Clinic says that the cholesterol levels of steroid users "are typically seen in much older persons with severe coronary stenosis who are awaiting bypass surgery."

Another study found that tablet forms of steroids can change the cholesterol levels within a week, but injected steroids had much less effect on cholesterol levels.

Steroids also cause water retention, which can lead to high blood pressure—another risk factor for heart attacks and stroke.

Animal experiments suggest that high doses of steroids can contribute to heart attacks and strokes in still another way. They increase the tendency of blood platelets to clump together, producing clots that may block a key blood vessel supplying the heart or brain.

Dr. Allan Levy, the team physician for the New York Giants and director of sports medicine at a U.S. Olympic treatment center, says, "We're seeing more and more fatal heart attacks in twenty-year-olds who are using steroids."

Effects on the Liver and Kidneys

The liver is the largest organ of the body, and also the most versatile—it has more than five hundred known functions! It secretes bile, which helps in the digestion of fats. It takes part in processing all the major food substances: proteins, carbohydrates, and fats. It stores various substances, including iron, glycogen (an animal starch), and vitamins A, B_{12}, and D. The liver also synthesizes important chemicals needed for blood clotting, destroys worn-out red blood cells, captures bacteria and other foreign particles in the blood, and detoxifies poisons and body wastes, eliminating their potential harmful effects. Steroids circulating through the body are carried to the liver and may be broken down or changed to less toxic forms. But when high doses of anabolic steroids are taken, cysts may develop as the liver becomes overworked. Steroids also decrease the flow of bile through the liver, which can increase the chances of a tumor developing. There have also been reports that ordinarily rare blood-filled sacs may develop in the livers of steroid users and can rupture and cause hemorrhaging.

Most frequent steroid-associated health problems cited by current and former users*

Problem	Percent
Liver disease	71%
Heart disease	56
Cancer	50
Shrinking of the testicles	49
Adverse personality changes	49
Death	45
Sterility	44
Kidney disease	38
Blood pressure problems	38
Stunted growth	36

*Respondents allowed more than one response

Some reasons cited by current users as to why they disagree with experts about risks of steroids*

Reasons	Percent
Not experiencing health problems themselves	87%
Other users not experiencing problems	80
Lack of "hard evidence"	54
Warnings are scare tactics	39
Experts were wrong in the past	27

*Responses from 45 current users; allowed more than one response

There have been at least three documented liver and kidney cancer deaths of athletes using steroids.

Some experts estimate that there have been over one hundred deaths of world-class athletes who used drugs to enhance their athletic performance in the last forty years.

Impurities, Infections, and AIDS

Another danger of steroid use is that the drugs may have been obtained from illegal sources. These black market drugs may or may not have the same ingredients as the licensed drugs—you're never sure what you're getting. Manufacturers of legal drugs have to meet strict standards. Illegal drug makers aren't as conscientious, and impurities can sometimes be dangerous, causing infections or serious side effects.

Some counterfeit steroids, for example, have been found to have high concentrations of cortisone, a different type of steroid, produced as a by-product when anabolic steroids are manufactured. The cortisone is removed in normal manufacturing because some people are allergic to it and could die from an injection. Cortisone can cause other severe side effects as well, even in people who are not allergic to it.

Many illegally used steroids come from veterinarians and were originally intended for use in animals. Regulations concerning animals' drugs are much less stringent, and the purity and strength may not be exact enough for human consumption. Strength variations can be dangerous. A user who takes a counterfeit steroid that is stronger than it is supposed to may unintentionally take an overdose. (Considering that athletes typically take huge doses to start with, the effects could be multiplied.) In addition, notes chemical dependency specialist Neil Carolan, "There are so many fakes on the market. One we sampled last summer was pure vegetable oil. There was no anabolic steroid at all."

Water-based steroids may contain microorganisms that can cause illness. Steroid users who inject steroids with a needle face even more potential hazards in the infections that can come from sharing needles or using needles that have not been properly sterilized. Richard

Sandlin, a world-ranked weight lifter and sports consultant, said that the college and pro football players he advised ". . . will do anything. They'll spend 50 bucks on some drugs, but they won't spend a quarter for a new syringe." Like IV heroin and cocaine abusers, steroid users may be placing themselves at risk for diseases like hepatitis and AIDS.

Steroids and Injuries

Some athletes who use steroids claim they use them to help prevent injuries. Most experts believe, however, that steroids help *cause* injuries! The Soviets were probably the first to use steroids in training. They have drastically cut down the use of them, and not just because of testing in international competitions. They have found that steroids cause injuries. According to Michael Yessis, an exercise physiologist who publishes *Soviet Sports Review* (a magazine that translates Soviet sports medicine articles into English), the Soviets found that steroids "are effective for getting bigger and stronger muscles, but the muscle grows so fast the ligament and tendon can't keep up with it." An article in the *Journal of the American Medical Association* in January 1987 noted, "It seems likely that their use may expose athletes to the risk of injury to ligaments and tendons and that these injuries may take longer to heal." Dr. Bertram Zarins, a sports medicine specialist at Massachusetts General Hospital and the New England Patriots football team physician, says, ". . . the general feeling is that with anabolic steroid use there are more major injuries, more major blowouts with steroids and a higher rate of injuries to others because someone weighs more and is more aggressive."

Psychological Effects

Aggressiveness is a commonly reported side effect of steroids. It may take the form of uncontrollable fits of aggression that have been called " 'roid rages" and "anabolic madness." Increased aggressiveness is beneficial to athletes in helping them to train harder, but when they take that aggression home with them, it can cause a lot of problems.

One steroid user described how he became uncontrollably angry when the driver of the car in front of him left his blinker on. The athlete got out at the next light and smashed in the other car's windshield. A woman bodybuilder described how she threw her husband against a door and couldn't stop hitting him again and again. Football player Dan Steinkuhler said that when he took steroids, "It made me feel real moody, violent. I wanted to kill somebody." Some murders have been committed by steroid users, and steroid testing in criminals will become more common. Dr. William Taylor of the American College of Sports Medicine believes that increased steroid use is linked with the rise in cases of date rape. "Here you have a drug that makes a person very aggressive," he says. "They don't know 'No' or boundaries, and they have a heightened sex drive. There's no question in my mind that there's a correlation."

"Cat on steroids!   Cat on steroids!!"

Steroid use can result in personality changes.

Some steroid users develop a psychological disorder often labeled "bodybuilders' psychosis." In one study, 10 percent of steroid-using bodybuilders suffered from hallucinations, more than 30 percent had manic episodes, and 5 percent were depressed. Sixty percent of women steroid users had an increased sex drive, and 80 percent of those women had had emotionally upsetting confrontations with family or friends since using steroids.

The researchers in that study, psychiatrists Harrison Pope, Jr., and David Katz, both of Harvard Medical School and McLean Hospital in Belmont, Massachusetts, report that one user deliberately drove his car into a tree at forty miles an hour while a friend videotaped him. Another user bought a $17,000 sports car he could not afford while he was taking steroids. When he stopped taking the drug, he realized how foolish he had been and sold the car. The next year, when he was taking steroids again, he went out and bought a $20,000 car. In most cases, when the steroid users stopped taking the drug, the symptoms went away. Dr. Katz believes that "these drugs disrupt the normal functioning of neurotransmitters in the central nervous system."

For some steroid users there are noticeable personality changes while they are using steroids and shortly afterward. Friends and family may notice that these changes occur cyclically because athletes often use steroids in cycles while they are training.

While taking steroids, some people experience feelings of higher self-esteem, higher levels of energy and mental intensity, greater tolerance to pain, greater sex drive, and increased appetite. But some find their sleeping patterns disturbed. Some steroid users become unable to accept failure, and they may be more inclined to use other drugs as well.

The periods of coming off steroids are the most dangerous for some users; the deep depression experienced during withdrawal from the drugs may lead to suicide.

References

Articles

Altman, Lawrence. "New 'Breakfast of Champions': A Recipe for Victory or Disaster?" *The New York Times,* November 20, 1988, pp. 1, 34.

Associated Press. "Study Finds Steroids Can Cause Psychotic Symptoms Among Athletes." *Star-Ledger* (Newark, N.J.), April 1, 1988, p. 1B.

Brody, Jane E. "Spreading Use of Steroids by Young Athletes Alarms Sports Medicine Specialists." *The New York Times.* February 18, 1988, p. B8.

Chelminski, Rudolph. "The Shocking Stain on International Athletics." *Reader's Digest,* August 1988, pp. 131–135.

Couzens, Gerald Secor. "Steroid Users Learn the Price of Success." *Star-Ledger,* (Newark, N.J.), March 5, 1989, p. 11.

Cowart, Virginia S. "Athletes and Steroids: The Bad Bargain." *Saturday Evening Post,* April 1987, pp. 56–59.

Fultz, Oliver. "'Roid Rage." *American Health,* May 1991, pp. 60–64.

Groves, David. "The Rambo Drug." *American Health,* September 1987, pp. 43–48.

Hecht, Anabel. "Anabolic Steroids: Pumping Trouble." *FDA Consumer,* September 1984, pp. 12–15.

Jackson, Lynn M. "Steroids Are as Addictive as Any Other Drug." *Courier-News* (Bridgewater, N.J.), May 3, 1991, p. B6.

Johnson, Karl. "Giants MD Lines Up on Side of Steroid Foes." *Star-Ledger* (Newark, N.J.), March 12, 1989, p. 15.

Lawn, John C. "Steroids: Playing With Trouble." *The Challenge,* November 1987, pp. 1–20.

Marshall, Eliot. "The Drug of Champions." *Science,* October 14, 1988, pp. 183–184.

Maugh, Thomas H., II. "Steroid Abuse: Turning Winners into Losers." *World Book Health and Medical Annual 1990,* Chicago: World Book, 1989, pp. 42–55.

Miller, Roger W. "Athletes and Steroids: Playing a Deadly Game," *FDA Consumer,* November 1987, pp. 17–21.

Rowan, Carl, and David Mazie. "The Mounting Menace of Steroids." *Reader's Digest,* February 1988, pp. 133–137.

Slothower, Jodie. "Mean Mental Muscles: The Psychological Price of Steroids." *Health,* January 1988, p. 20.

Stehlin, Dori. "For Athletes and Dealers, Black Market Steroids Are Risky Business." *FDA Consumer,* September 1987, pp. 24–25.

Taylor, William N. "Super Athletes Made to Order." *Psychology Today,* May 1985, pp. 63–66.

Taylor, William N. "Anabolic Steroids." *DATAFAX Information Series,* October 1989, pp. 1–4.

"Teenagers Blasé About Steroid Use." *FDA Consumer,* December 1990, pp. 2–3.

Toufexis, Anastasia. "Shortcut to the Rambo Look." *Time,* January 30, 1989, p. 78.

Books

Goldman, Bob. *Death in the Locker Room.* South Bend, Ind.: Icarus Press, 1984.

Mohun, Janet. *Drugs, Steroids, and Sports.* New York: Franklin Watts, 1988.

Nuwer, Hank. *Steroids.* New York: Franklin Watts, 1990.

Wadler, Gary I., and Brian Hainline. *Drugs and the Athlete.* F. A. Davis, Philadelphia: 1989.

Pamphlets

American College of Sports Medicine. *Anabolic Steroids and Athletes.*

Bartimole, John. *Drugs and the Athlete . . . a Losing Combination.* National Collegiate Athletic Association, 1988.

Newsom, Mary Margaret, ed., *Drug Free: U.S. Olympic Committee Drug Education Handbook, 1989–92.*

Peterson, Robert C. *The Use of Steroids in Sports Can Be Dangerous.* National Clearinghouse for Alcohol and Drug Information, September 1988 (MS391), pp. 1–5.

United States General Accounting Office. *Drug Misuse: Anabolic Steroids and Human Growth Hormone.* August, 1989.

6

The Criminal Connection

Using steroids without a prescription is illegal, but at least $100 million worth of black market steroids are sold each year. In most cases, steroids are as easy to obtain as other drugs, such as cocaine and heroin.

Where Do People Get Steroids?

Drug experts estimate that about 20 percent of the steroids used by athletes are prescribed by doctors, although this percentage may decrease now that steroids have been classified as "controlled drugs" by the federal Drug Enforcement Administration. The other 80 percent are obtained illegally from black market sources. According to the Justice Department, about one-third of the steroids bought in the United States are illegally imported from other countries (mostly from Mexico, but also from European and South American nations), one-third are counterfeit steroids, made in unlicensed underground labs in the United States, and one-third are made legally for other purposes but find their way into the black market.

In the past, athletes and bodybuilders were the only ones who used steroids. They got them from other athletes, or from their coaches or from doctors or pharmacists who didn't mind bending the rules to "help" the athletes compete better. Many users got them from members of gyms and fitness clubs where they worked out. Another major source was from veterinarians who gave athletes steroids used for racehorses.

By the early 1980s, more than a dozen different kinds of steroids could be ordered through the mail from ads for "special vitamin preparations" in weight-lifting magazines and mail-order catalogs. Now, however, crime syndicates are much more involved in steroids as well. New Jersey Representative William Hughes testified before the House of Representatives, saying, "Children using steroids are exposed to the syndicates that push amphetamines, cocaine, heroin, and marijuana."

Ironically, this situation was the indirect result of efforts to bring the steroid problem under control. In 1985, the Food and Drug Administration (FDA) took several steroids off the market, including one of the most popular, Dianabol. Until that time, steroids were most often obtained from a doctor's prescription or through underground channels that obtained legal drugs. But with the elimination of these legal steroids, black market distributors turned more to underground laboratories and foreign- manufactured steroids.

When steroids are smuggled into the country from Mexico and Europe, they are then sold through mail catalogs or in gyms and health clubs. In other countries, like Mexico, a prescription is not needed to buy steroids, and they are often quite cheap. A bottle of Dianabol that can be bought for $5 in Tijuana usually sells for about $50 on the streets in the United States. Steroids are smuggled into the United States in automobiles that are driven across the border or by couriers (called mules) who find routes taken by illegal aliens.

Drug dealers have realized there is a lot of money to be made in steroids. Many dealers find $100,000 per transaction is the minimum they can buy from distributors. As Assistant U.S. Attorney in San Diego Phillip Halpern points out, one of the unfortunate things about prosecuting the "amateur" steroid traffickers—athletes and other "nice guys" who thought they were doing athletes a service—is that it opens up the door to professional cocaine and heroin dealers who realize there is a lot of money to be made with steroids. Mr. Halpern says that it is not uncommon to find gym bags containing hundreds of thousands of dollars passed in a steroid sale.

Legal Penalties

In the early 1980, the government did not realize how widespread steroid use was. Trafficking penalties for steroids were not clear, and they were substantially less than those for trafficking other drugs. Often there was just a fine of $500 to $1000. And yet there was just as much money to be made selling steroids as "hard drugs."

The Department of Justice began investigating illegal manufacturing and selling of steroids in 1985. Now the FDA, the FBI, the Customs Service, and the Department of Justice are working together to stop the sale of steroids. More than $12 million worth of steroids have been confiscated, and more than 150 people have been indicted for selling steroids. Before 1984, no one had ever been prosecuted for illegal steroid distribution or manufacture.

One of the first steroid rings that was discovered was shipping the steroids from Tijuana, Mexico into San Diego, California. Thirty-four people were indicted, including a British Olympic athlete, David Jenkins, and Dan Duchaine, the author of *The Underground Steroid Handbook*. The drug ring was said to be selling $70 million worth of steroids each year. After David Jenkins received a seven-year sentence, U.S. District Judge Lawrence J. Irving said, "Hopefully the message will get out that illegal (steroid) trafficking will not be tolerated in the United States of America." But when that drug ring was shut down, copycat operations began springing up.

Crackdown efforts to stop steroid use have come a long way. Several underground labs in the United States that manufacture steroids have been shut down since the mid-1980s. But more just keep popping up. Experts believe there may be up to twenty additional American underground laboratories manufacturing steroids.

In the late 1980s, a growing number of states tightened up their laws. In 1987, California classified steroids as controlled substances, which made prosecution much easier. Alabama, Florida, and North Carolina also classified these drugs as controlled substances, and a number of other states passed laws changing possession of anabolic steroids from a misdemeanor to a felony. This change meant that not only could a person go to jail for illegal use of steroids, but also distributors of the drugs could have any property purchased with the profits of drug sales—a health spa or gym, for example—confiscated by the government.

The federal government also took a big step forward in 1988, when the Omnibus Anti-Substance Abuse Act made the distribution or possession of steroids with intent to sell them without a prescription a felony, punishable by three years in prison and a heavy fine. Selling to minors could bring a sentence of up to six years in prison. Tracking down and prosecuting steroid traffickers, however, still had a lower priority in government efforts than those involved in controlled substances such as heroin and cocaine. Many people felt this situation should change, including Gene Haislip, a federal Drug Enforcement Administration official, who testified that "Steroids constitute a growing threat to our national health and safety." Congress responded, and early in 1991 the Anabolic Steroids Control Act of 1990 took effect, making twenty-seven anabolic steroids controlled substances.

Now the DEA is actively involved in enforcing the laws regulating steroid use. But there are still some difficulties. For one thing, U.S. Customs agents' dogs are not able to sniff out steroids as they can other drugs like heroin and cocaine.

What Should Be Done?

Fighting the steroid epidemic is turning out to be rather complicated. Experts suggest several ways to tackle the problem. Dr. Charles E.

Yesalis, who collaborated with Dr. William Buckley on the Penn State study that determined the high level of adolescent steroid use, suggests several avenues of attacking the problem:

1. Putting more money into prosecuting steroid pushers

2. Improving steroid education

3. Putting money into drug testing in high schools

4. Changing society's focus on winning to a focus on the thrill of competition

Increasing Steroid Prosecution. Dr. Yesalis points out that increasing prosecution of traffickers ends up increasing the crime syndicates' involvement in steroids.

Education. Arresting the people who manufacture and distribute steroids is only half the problem. As long as there are people who want to buy the drugs, new dealers will spring up. That's why many experts believe that educating people about steroids is so important. "Kids and adults are using these drugs without knowing what they're all about," says Dr. Stuart Nightingale, associate commissioner for health affairs at the FDA.

The FDA and the Department of Education have been trying to increase public awareness about steroids by sending newsletters and posters to grade schools across the nation. One poster, for example, shows professional wrestler Jesse Ventura telling kids, "Don't Pump Trouble . . . Stay Away From Steroids."

But Dr. Yesalis points out that steroid education attempts often fail because no tests of long-term effects have ever been conducted. Tobacco, alcohol, and "hard drug" education is somewhat effective because there are many proven harmful effects. There are very few proven studies of long-term effects of steroids, although there are a lot of clinical indications of possible effects. In addition, it is hard to change a person's behavior when there are definite perceived benefits to something, and steroids do seem to change a person's appearance and strength in some cases. Dr. Yesalis also points out a steroid education program in Oregon that backfired. Football players who learned about steroids from the seminars were even more inclined to take the drug!

Random Steroid Testing. Some gyms in the country have declared war on steroids. In many weight-lifting competitions, the competitors must undergo drug testing. Olympic athletes must undergo testing, but other sports are not as strict. Many individuals, groups, and organizations such as the National High School Athletic Coaches Association believe that random drug testing should be done in high school athletic programs to scare kids out of taking steroids. Kids don't listen to reports about harmful effects, so there needs to be some other

Team Up Against Steroids

"Team up against steroids," urges a poster from the U.S. Department of Education.

fear about consequences of steroid use, they say. Disqualification from competition can be a very strong deterrent.

But, as Dr. Yesalis points out, there are many things to consider when discussing the issue of random drug testing. It would be very expensive (a single drug test costs about $200), and most schools are struggling financially as it is. Many legal questions about invasion of privacy would undoubtedly arise. In addition, many students do not use steroids while participating in sports, so random testing of high school athletes would have no effect on deterring the use of steroids "to look good."

Changing Our "Play to Win" Values. Competing to win is a value that is deeply ingrained in our culture and virtually impossible to change. Any change in the attitude of a whole society takes many years to come about.

Some experts take the pessimistic view that we will never be able to get rid of steroids. Anabolic steroid expert James E. Wright, research director at the Adirondack Mountain Foundation, says, "The use of anabolic steroids is too consistent with societal values—bigger, stronger, taller, faster—to be eradicated."

Still, it is equally unlikely that governments and individuals will stop trying to bring the steroid problem under control. Dr. Yesalis suggests that random drug testing is the method that would yield the most results, although it would be very expensive. For now, until officials can come up with a sure-fire plan of attack, those fighting against steroid use are doing so on all four battlefronts.

References

Articles

Brody, Jane E. "Spreading Use of Steroids by Young Athletes Alarms Sports Medicine Specialists." *The New York Times,* February 18, 1988, p. B8.

Brubaker, Bill. "Players Close Eyes to Steroids' Risks." *Washington Post,* February 1, 1987, pp. C1, C13.

Kahler, Kathryn. "Steroids 'Mania' Spawning Perilous New Drug Traffic." *Star-Ledger* (Newark, N.J.), January 8, 1989, pp. 1, 29.

Marshall, Eliot. "The Drug of Champions." *Science,* October 14, 1988, pp. 183–184.

Miller, Roger W. "Athletes and Steroids: Playing a Deadly Game." *FDA Consumer,* November 1987, pp. 17–21.

Mirkin, Gabe. "Hormonal Helpers." *Health,* March 1984, pp. 6, 46.

Modeland, Vern. "Putting Pressure on Illegal Steroid Traffic." *FDA Consumer,* October 1989, pp. 33–34.

Penn, Stanley, "As Ever More People Try Anabolic Steroids, Traffickers Take Over." *Wall Street Journal,* October 4, 1988, p. 1.

Rowan, Carl, and David Mazie. "The Mounting Menace of Steroids." *Reader's Digest,* February 1988, pp. 133–137.

Stehlin, Dori. "For Athletes and Dealers, Black Market Steroids Are Risky Business." *FDA Consumer,* September 1987, pp. 24–25.

Weaver, Warren Jr. "U.S. Detecting Gain on Steroid Abuse." *The New York Times,* December 11, 1988, p. 35.

Yesalis, Charles. "Steroid Use Is Not Just an Adult Problem." *The New York Times,* December 4, 1988, p. 12.

Books

Nuwer, Hank. *Steroids.* New York: Franklin Watts, 1990.

7

Steroids in Sports

The steroid problem first began among athletes who wanted to improve their performance and coaches who were trying to help them, not realizing the potential dangers. Although steroid use has now spread into the general population, it is still most common in the sports world.

Athletes were faced with enormous pressure to do well. Bill Curry, football coach at Alabama, comments, "The system is saying do whatever it takes to win. It is saying, 'We'll make you rich, famous and put you on TV.' We are a quick-fix society that wants the rush, that medal, that national championship."

Athletes who use steroids don't think of themselves as cheaters. Many set high goals for themselves and work hard at achieving them. Steroids are seen as just a way to help them work harder and more effectively. But the athletes who don't use steroids feel that steroid users have an unfair advantage.

U.S. shot-putter Augie Wolf summed up many athletes' feelings: "Drug taking is rampant. Only the uninformed get caught. The pressure to take drugs is enormous. An athlete asks himself, 'Do I take drugs and win medals, or do I play fair and finish last'?"

A Widespread Problem

In some sports, such as power lifting, some athletes believe they have to use steroids in order to keep up with everyone else. Gaby Bussmann, a West German Olympic team runner, switched her event from a 400-meter race to an 800-meter race because she believed that many of the athletes competing in the 400-meter event took steroids, and they had an unfair advantage. "There are some disciplines where it is difficult to qualify for the Olympics without drugs," she declared.

Steroid use in "power" events such as weight lifting, shot put, discus, and javelin, as well as sprinting events, has been known for a long time, but it has also been discovered in such Olympic sports as bobsledding, softball, and cycling. According to Dr. Robert Voy, former director of Sports Medicine and Science for the U.S. Olympic Committee, the only Olympic events that have not yet reported steroid abusers are women's field hockey and synchronized swimming. "I

don't think there are many sports in which increased strength and aggressiveness wouldn't be an advantage," he says.

Animal Drugging

Not only human athletes are using steroids and other drugs to enhance their athletic performance. Drug use is often a part of the competitive world of horse racing as well.

In 1986, Precisionist was a candidate for horse of the year. He retired from racing the following year and was sent to Florida to begin his new career, fathering the next generation of racehorses. But when the results of Precisionist's first season at stud were in, breeders were dismayed. More than 40 percent of the mares whose owners had paid for the thoroughbred's stud services failed to become pregnant. Precisionist was given a fertility test—and he flunked!

What was especially alarming was that this was not a single, isolated incident. A study conducted by the University of Pennsylvania on 852 stallions found that nearly a quarter of them had low sperm counts and performed poorly in their first year at stud. (Even the famous champion Secretariat suffered from similar problems in the first year after he retired from racing.)

Veterinarians say that the stresses of training can cause these problems. But a widespread contributing factor seems to be the use of steroids. Although these drugs are illegal or strictly regulated in most states, many racehorse owners and trainers use them in secret. Anabolic steroids provide important short-term benefits: They help horses to gain weight and to recover more quickly from injuries. With the high prize money to be won in races, the long-term drawbacks— hormonal effects that can harm the horse's breeding ability for at least a year—may seem worth the gamble. The University of Pennsylvania report concluded that steroid use "is an open secret and an almost accepted part of the sport." Yet $3 to $4 million in stud fees can be lost during the year it takes for steroid-treated horses to recover their breeding ability.

Many of Alysheba's wins were achieved under the influence of the drug Lasix.

Not a New Problem

Ironically, the popularity of steroid use in sports was an indirect result of efforts to curb the use of other drugs. Stimulants such as amphetamines had become widespread in athletics since the end of World War II. The athletes took the drugs to gain an extra energy boost.

When drug testing was set up for the first time in the 1968 Winter Olympics, drug-using athletes began to look for alternatives that would not be as easy to detect. Steroids seemed an ideal choice because they helped to build a stronger body rather than to give a quick extra boost. Their use could be stopped long before a competitive event, so no traces would show up by the time the tests were taken.

A 1974 Senate subcommittee report concluded that amphetamines and steroids were the most commonly abused drugs in amateur athletics.

In 1975, the International Olympic Committee (IOC) ruled that athletes could not use steroids or other "doping" techniques because they might give an unfair advantage to those who use them. They are considered performance-enhancing drugs—substances that enable athletes to perform beyond their natural abilities. IOC-banned drugs include anabolic steroids (as well as testosterone and growth hormones), beta blockers and diuretics, blood doping (injecting extra oxygen-carrying red blood cells), narcotics (including codeine, heroin, and morphine), and stimulants (including amphetamines, cocaine, and even high doses of caffeine). Legal drugs that are used to "mask" or hide illegal drugs are also banned. Today about 3,000 drugs are on the IOC's banned list. Other sports organizations have their own lists of banned drugs, although most are based on the IOC list.

In the United States and most other countries, taking performance-enhancing drugs is not necessarily against the law, unless the specific drug is illegal. But some countries, such as Belgium, France, and Greece, have passed stiff national laws banning the use of drugs in sports.

In the world of professional sports, drug testing is often up to the individual sports association. The National Basketball Association began drug testing in 1983. Baseball drug testing began in 1986. Wimbledon and U.S. Open tennis players were also tested beginning in 1986. In 1986, when the National Collegiate Athletic Association (NCAA) first ordered steroid testing for those who were participating in the post-season football bowl games, twenty players were disqualified, including star linebacker Brian Bosworth. Bosworth was outraged. "I'll continue to fight against the abuse of drugs," he declared, ". . . recreational drugs that are destroying society. Steroids aren't destroying society." But many people believe steroids make competition unfair. The NFL (National Football League) checked for steroids in 1987 for the first time and set standards for steroid levels. A positive test result would suspend a player for thirty days. Two additional positive readings could result in expulsion from the league.

Defensive end Roland Barbay was banned from playing in the Sugar Bowl by the NCAA after a drug test detected steroids.

The first steroid suspensions in the NFL came in 1989, when thirteen players failed the league's tests for steroid use.

The punishments for those caught using illegal drugs usually depend on the athletic organization. Some believe that athletes should be banned for life. Other organizations ban the entire team an athlete belongs to. The IOC currently suspends athletes who are caught using banned drugs: for three years the first time, and for life if they are caught again. When athletes "accidentally" take too much caffeine, codeine, or other everyday drugs. they can be banned for three months, then two years if they do it again, and for life if they are caught a third time.

Is Steroid Use in Sports Increasing?

Although awareness of steroid use is growing, testing is increasing, and penalties are becoming stiffer, many believe these measures have not been very effective in reducing the use of these drugs in sports.

When an Olympic gold medal was taken away from Canadian sprinter Ben Johnson in 1988, he lost an estimated $10–15 million in endorsement contracts, and he was suspended from international competition for two years. His trainer had urged him to take steroids because "the whole world" was taking them.

At the 1988 Olympic games, eight steroid users were caught, and eight athletes dropped out rather than be tested. In 1989, superstar athlete Carl Lewis told a congressional subcommittee that he believed up to ten 1988 Olympic medals were won by athletes who had used steroids. Some experts believe that as many as half of the 9,000 who competed had used steroids some time during their training for the Olympics. Male athletes aren't the only ones using steroids, either. Professor Wildor Hollmann, president of the World Federation of Sports Medicine in Cologne, declared, "I believe that today there are few women's world records in running, high jump, broad jump, shot put, discus, and possibly javelin that have come about without the help of anabolic steroids."

The number of steroid-positive urine samples found at Seoul in 1988 was roughly the same as in Los Angeles in 1984, but most experts believe steroids are being used by even more athletes than ever. The athletes have just learned better ways to avoid getting caught. Ben Johnson was simply one of the few who were caught because they didn't stop using the drug in time.

"For an athlete to test positive in the Olympic Games means something has gone wrong," explains Dr. Robert Voy, director of Sports Medicine and Science for the U.S. Olympic Committee. "It's like the embezzler. The embezzler gets along fine until he gets a little greedy, and then he takes a little bit more and then a little bit more until something goes awry."

Ten athletes were disqualified because of drugs that were banned, including steroids. Twenty others tested positive but were not disqualified because levels of drugs detected were not high enough. (Some drugs are illegal when detected in any quantity; others must be found above a certain limit set by the IOC.)

A positive test for a banned substance is not the final word. The Olympic rules provide athletes with several layers of appeal. Three separate levels of officials evaluate a positive test result by voting whether or not they believe the drug was taken for performance enhancement. There have been rumors that politics may have played a role in some decisions. Also, sometimes an appeal is won on a technicality, even if the player was guilty.

In other amateur organizations and in professional sports, many believe steroid use is still on the rise, as well. The NFL reported in 1987 and 1988 that 6 percent of its players tested positive for steroids, but many experts believe these numbers are greatly underestimated. Announcement of decreases in drug use may not necessarily be a sign that drug use has dropped. For example, at the UCLA laboratory that does drug testing for the NCAA, Dr. Donald Catlin, chief of the drug-testing lab, found an apparent drop in drug use from 2.5 percent to 0.5 percent over a two-year span. "But we found that the users were merely changing from oil-based steroids, which are long-acting, to water-based steroids, which are short-acting." The water-based steroids are washed out of the body more quickly and can be stopped closer to the testing time, so fewer athletes were caught.

How Is Drug Testing Done?

Current drug testing is usually done with a urine sample. When a person takes a drug, it is broken down by the body, and some of it is absorbed. But some of it may be excreted in the urine. Or some of the breakdown products of the drug (called metabolites) might pass into the urine. Drug tests check urine samples for a particular drug or its metabolites, which can show up in the urine days or sometimes even weeks after the drug was taken.

Two techniques are commonly used for drug tests: gas chromatography and mass spectrometry. These tests are very accurate, but they require complex equipment and are expensive. For some drugs, testing has to be conducted for four or five different metabolites. Drug tests in the United States usually cost about $200.

To obtain the urine samples for testing, the athlete is observed while urinating into a container that is divided into two vials, both of which are sealed by the athlete. Samples are then identified by a number code, not with the athlete's name. The first sample is tested. If there is a positive result, the other specimen is then tested while qualified observers watch.

At the Olympic Games, and typically at other major international events, the first three finishers in each event are tested for illegal drugs. Random testing is also becoming a common practice. Just before an event, several athletes are chosen randomly. Right after the event, they are told to go to the testing station. If they refuse, they are considered guilty and will be disqualified.

Getting Around the Drug Tests

Olympic testing officials are constantly trying to keep up with the latest technological developments in illegal drug use among athletes.

67

The drug tests are becoming more sensitive and better at detecting drugs longer after their use has been discontinued. Scientists can now detect traces of steroids in urine samples with a concentration of one part per billion. Only a short while ago, athletes thought that stanozolol, the steroid that Ben Johnson was caught using, was undetectable. Johnson had actually been using the drug since 1981. His positive test result was detected with an extremely sensitive test first developed in 1985 and therefore not available at the 1984 Olympics.

Dr. Donald Catlin, the director of the UCLA Olympic Analytical Laboratory and director of drug testing at the 1984 Olympics, said there is "nothing magical" about the way athletes can beat the system. "Testing is by no means foolproof. It can't, and never will, catch everyone. The best we can hope for is that regular testing will lead to a decrease in drug use—and a growing awareness that aside from being unfair, drugs can literally kill the users."

Athletes who use drugs are constantly trying to keep ahead of the drug-testing officials. "Athletes know how to beat the system," says Dr. Robert Voy. The easiest way around steroid testing is to use the drugs while training, then stop long before competition. This is what most steroid-using athletes do. They can continue using steroids until as few as ten to fourteen days before urine tests are conducted—and athletes get plenty of notice about testing, especially in the United States, where the Constitution protects citizens against illegal search and seizure.

Some athletes claim that drug-using athletes can easily bribe officials into swapping urine samples so that they will test negative for drug use.

Certain drugs can hide evidence of steroids in urine samples. Diuretics, for example, cause a person to urinate more than usual. With the body producing more urine, the drug traces in any particular sample will be more diluted by water and less likely to be picked up in tests. In 1987, drug-testing laboratories noticed that some urine samples contained a drug called probenecid. After researching this

68

drug, they discovered that it keeps steroids from entering the urine. The IOC now bans probenecid and other masking drugs and requires any athlete whose urine sample appears to have been diluted to be retested.

Many illegal techniques involve taking substances that are normally found in the body—testosterone, for example. But there are tests to detect such practices. To test for extra testosterone, the amount of this hormone is measured and compared to the amount of another hormone, epitestosterone. A high testosterone ratio shows that the athletes took illegal supplements of the natural substance. Similarly, other tests check for illegal use of growth hormones and blood doping.

Scientists are working on tests that measure the profile of hormones; they believe that these could indicate the use of anabolic steroids, even when no steroids or metabolites can be detected.

In addition to all of the techniques for "fooling" drug tests, experts believe that athletes may be using as many as a dozen different performance-enhancing drugs that are not yet detectable by current drug tests. "The athletes are ahead of us and have stuff we don't even know about," says Dr. Voy. "Our testing . . . has simply not solved the problem."

Random Drug Testing

Officials feel that drug use in sports has gotten out of hand. At the 1987 Zurich World Class, the most prestigious one-day meet for track and field, more than half of the twenty-eight athletes who were scheduled to compete in shot put, hammer, javelin, and discus events did not show up after they found out there would be testing for steroids. The organizer of the meet, Res Bruger, declared, "This can only mean that doping tests scared them off. If things go on this way, we won't stage such events in the future." The same thing happened at a Los Angeles competition in 1988. When athletes were notified there would be random drug testing, so many people withdrew from the competition that the shot put and discus events had to be cancelled.

At major competitions like the Olympics, where athletes know they will be severely penalized for positive tests for drugs, very few test positive. (The average positive rate at the Olympics, for example, is less than 0.5 percent.) However, tests at international competitions where the athletes knew there would be no punishments, produced positive tests for up to 50 percent of the competitors!

Many countries are urging that random testing any time during the season be adopted by all international sports competitive organizations. With random testing all year round, drug use during training can be detected, and perhaps drug use would be less common. The International Amateur Athletic Foundation, which governs international athletics around the world, is trying to work out a fair way of conducting year-round random tests for all international sports.

The world is moving toward better controls over steroid and other drug use in athletics. In 1988, sports officials from twenty-nine countries met in Sweden to discuss ways to control the use of anabolic steroids among athletes. Their conclusion was that year-round random testing during training, with disqualification for drug users, would be the best solution.

An anti-doping charter was adopted by the IOC in 1988 and was approved by the United Nations Educational, Scientific, and Cultural Organization (UNESCO) at a meeting in Moscow. An international group, including members from Britain, Canada, Germany, the Council of Europe, Norway, the Soviet Union, and the United States, is now working toward getting nations and international sports federations to adopt the charter and to begin programs to discourage drug doping.

The United States and the Soviet Union have also been negotiating on the testing of each other's athletes. Such a program would counter claims on both sides that countries are covering up their athletes' drug use. When an agreement has been reached between the two countries' Olympic committees, other countries would also be invited to be a part of the agreement.

International Olympic Committee president Juan Antonio Samaranch is urging that an international commission be formed that would drop in unannounced to test athletes all around the world. "The most important step must be to have an international commission going around the world during training time, entering different countries without any kind of restrictions."

Some countries have already adopted year-round random testing. In Sweden, for example, athletes must submit to tests at any time, and refusal is taken as failing the drug test. Germany, Bulgaria, and Great Britain are all moving to stricter testing policies.

In the United States, random drug testing inevitably brings up Constitutional questions. Dr. Voy believes that if surprise testing cannot be attained because of legal problems, the next best solution would be testing on one-day notice. Short-notice testing is an effective method because it doesn't give the athletes enough time to stop using steroids.

Some experts are calling for an international declaration of anabolic steroids, as well testosterone, HCG (human chorionic gonadotropin), and HGH (human growth hormone), as controlled substances. This would make their use without a prescription illegal and would cause pharmaceutical companies to put tighter controls on their production and use.

All around the world, proposals are being made and policies are being adopted to help eliminate drugs from sports.

References

Articles

Associated Press. "Study Finds Steroids Can Cause Psychotic Symptoms Among Athletes." *Star-Ledger* (Newark, N.J.), April 1, 1988, p. 1B.

Axthelm, Pete. "Using Chemistry to Get the Gold." *Newsweek,* July 25, 1988, pp. 62–63.

———. "The Doped-Up Games." *Newsweek,* October 10, 1988, pp. 54–56.

Brody, Jane E. "Spreading Use of Steroids by Young Athletes Alarms Sports Medicine Specialists." *The New York Times,* February 18, 1988, p. B8.

Brower, Montgomery, and Carol Azizian. "Steroids Built Mike Keys Up; Then They Tore Him Down." *People,* March 20, 1989, pp. 107–108.

Brubaker, Bill. "Players Close Eyes to Steroids' Risks." *Washington Post,* February 1, 1987, pp. C1, C13.

Chelminski, Rudolph. "The Shocking Stain on International Athletics." *Reader's Digest,* August 1988, pp. 131–135.

Cowart, Virginia S. "Athletes and Steroids: The Bad Bargain." *Saturday Evening Post,* April 1987, pp. 56–59.

Holmes, John. "Squeezing the Drugs from Athletics." *Insight,* December 26, 1988, pp. 46–47.

Janofsky, Michael. "System Accused of Failing Test Posed by Drugs." *The New York Times,* November 17, 1988, pp. A1, D31.

———. "Victory at Any Cost: Drug Pressure Growing." *The New York Times,* November 21, 1988, pp. 1, C13.

Johnson, Karl. "Giants MD Lines Up on Side of Steroid Foes." *Star-Ledger* (Newark, N.J.), March 12, 1989, p. 15.

Marshall, Eliot. "The Drug of Champions." *Science,* October 14, 1988, pp. 183–184.

Maugh, Thomas H., II. "Steroid Abuse: Turning Winners into Losers." *World Book Health and Medical Annual 1990,* Chicago: World Book, 1989, pp. 42–55.

Miller, Roger W. "Athletes and Steroids: Playing a Deadly Game." *FDA Consumer,* November 1987, pp. 17–21.

Books

Goldman, Bob. *Death in the Locker Room.* South Bend, Ind.: Icarus Press, 1984.

Mohun, Janet. *Drugs, Steroids, and Sports.* New York: Franklin Watts, 1988.

Nuwer, Hank. *Steroids.* New York: Franklin Watts, 1990.

Wadler, Gary I., and Brian Hainline. *Drugs and the Athlete.* Philadelphia: F. A. Davis, 1989.

Pamphlets

American College of Sports Medicine. *Anabolic Steroids and Athletes.*

Bartimole, John. *Drugs and the Athlete . . . a Losing Combination.* National Collegiate Athletic Association, 1988.

Newsom, Mary Margaret, ed. *Drug Free: U.S. Olympic Committee Drug Education Handbook, 1989–92.*

Peterson, Robert C. *The Use of Steroids in Sports Can Be Dangerous.* National Clearinghouse for Alcohol and Drug Information, September 1988 (MS391), pp. 1–5.

United States General Accounting Office. *Drug Misuse: Anabolic Steroids and Human Growth Hormone.* August 1989.

8

—

Other Performance Drugs

Athletes have always tried to find ways to increase their athletic performance. Some search for a new diet plan, better training equipment, or better shoes. Drugs and other substances to enhance performance have also been used by some athletes for a long time. In the third century B.C., some Greek athletes who competed in the first Olympic games ate mushrooms and herbs to give themselves a boost. At the turn of the century, Vin Muriani was advertised as the wine for athletes and was supposedly used by French cyclists and a lacrosse team in Peru. The special formula was a mixture of coca leaf extract (cocaine comes from the coca plant) and wine. In the 1904 Olympics, American athlete Thomas Hicks won the marathon after taking a cocktail with strychnine and brandy.

There are many different kinds of drugs used in sports that are banned because they may help athletes to perform beyond their natural abilities and therefore might give them an unfair advantage.

These performance drugs and their effects include:

—*Stimulants* make a person more alert and sometimes give a high feeling.

—*Anabolic steroids* help build up muscle tissue.

—Other *hormonal growth promoters* also stimulate muscle and other body tissue development.

—*Painkillers*—these are much more powerful than everyday pain remedies like aspirin and can help an athlete push farther than the normal pain barrier would naturally allow.

—*Anti-inflammatory drugs* reduce pain and swelling.

—*Beta blockers* are normally used for people with heart conditions and are sometimes used by athletes to calm their nerves.

—*Diuretics* are used by some athletes to lose water weight to qualify for a lower weight class or to dilute urine samples to make it harder to detect the use of other drugs.

Stimulants

Stimulants have traditionally been the most abused drugs in sports because, when taken before a competitive event, they give a boost of energy that allows athletes to try harder. Stimulants include such controlled substances as amphetamines and cocaine, but they also include common ingredients in cold medicines. Even caffeine, which is found in tea, coffee, cola drinks, and chocolate, is a stimulant.

Stimulants often give a feeling of extra energy, but when the effect wears off, the users often feel wiped out and depressed. Stimulants can make the user feel more aggressive, high, and less concerned with pain sensations.

Amphetamines have a long history of abuse in sports. These drugs stimulate a release of adrenaline into the blood, which causes the heart to beat faster and the blood pressure to rise, bringing a feeling of alertness. Actually, however, the amphetamine user's reflexes are

75

decreased, and a reduced awareness of pain may increase the risk of injury. Amphetamines used to be prescribed for narcolepsy, an illness that causes people to fall asleep suddenly, at any time. Later, amphetamines were also prescribed as an appetite suppressant for people who wanted to lose weight. However, today amphetamines are controlled substances because of all their side effects, including a potential for addiction.

In the 1980s, cocaine became the drug of choice. It has been estimated that as many as one in fifteen Americans have tried this drug, and during the eighties there were a number of headline stories about cocaine use by some of the biggest sports stars. Cocaine is used in sports by some athletes because it helps players forget about pain, which allows them to play harder. But cocaine use can cause nosebleeds as the drug damages the tissue in the nose; it can also disturb the natural rhythm of the heart, which can result in a heart

"I THINK THEY'RE HIGH FOR THIS GAME IN MORE WAYS THAN ONE!"

attack. During the 1980s, several athletes died of heart attacks caused by cocaine.

Amphetamines and cocaine are illegal drugs, but some stimulants are banned for sports use even though they are perfectly legal. SMAs (sympathomimetic amines) are drugs that can be found in cold medicines. They include ephedrine, phenylpropanolamine, and pseudoephedrine. They speed up the heartbeat and cause some blood vessels to widen and others to narrow. (Their decongestant action, which helps relieve cold symptoms, is the result of constriction of the blood vessels in the nasal lining.) Because these drugs can be purchased in a supermarket without a prescription, some athletes take them for extra pep. Large quantities of caffeine (the equivalent of about ten cups of coffee) are also banned for sports use because in excessive amounts caffeine, too, can give players an added boost.

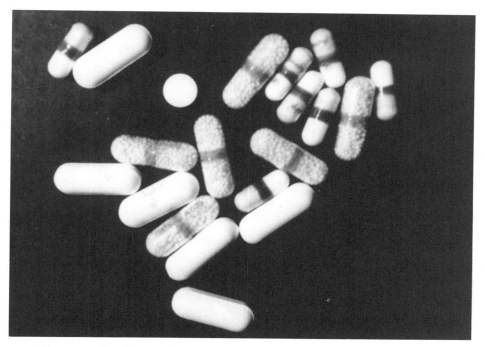

Even some legal, over-the-counter drugs contain stimulants that are banned from sports.

Stimulants are especially dangerous because they may raise a person's exhaustion threshold. The body feels exhaustion as a defense against damaging overstimulation. Dizziness, aching muscles, shortness of breath, and a racing heart are signs that you should slow down. Stimulants like amphetamines can speed the body up too much and cause an athlete to push himself or herself far beyond the normal limits. Sometimes this exertion can cause an athlete to collapse, or even die.

Drugs like amphetamines are also addictive. The user develops a tolerance to the drug and needs larger amounts to get the same effects. Stopping the drug produces feelings of depression, as well as unpleasant (and possibly dangerous) physical withdrawal symptoms.

Human Growth Hormone

Stimulants are easy to detect with drug tests because they are taken right before an event and can be found in high concentrations in blood or urine samples. Steroids were turned to because they can be discontinued long enough before an event so that they will not be detected. Some athletes are turning to "natural" body substances to give them an extra boost. The use of these substances and techniques is much harder to detect because there is nothing "foreign" to discover in a drug test.

Human growth hormone (HGH or hGH) is normally produced in the pituitary gland, found inside the brain. It stimulates growth and also helps to control various reactions involved in the body's metabolism. HGH is used legally to help children who are lacking sufficient amounts of this vital hormone. Without it their growth will be stunted. Some people have the opposite disorder: they produce too much growth hormone. Such a person may become a giant, reaching over seven feet tall. An overproduction of HGH is often due to a tumor in the pituitary gland. When this happens after normal growth has stopped, the result is a condition called acromegaly, in which the hands, feet, nose, lips, and other body parts become grossly enlarged. The heart, too, may be affected, which can lead to congestive heart failure.

Excess production of human growth hormone can result in giantism. Robert Wadlow, 8 feet 8½ inches tall, is shown here at age twenty-one with his normal-sized parents, brothers, and sisters.

Until fairly recently, HGH was produced by extracting it from the pituitary glands of people who had died. In the mid-1980s, however, scientists were able to synthesize it in the laboratory, and later the process was developed on a commercial scale. This is good news for children lacking the natural hormone. But it also makes HGH more accessible to those who want to increase their size. In addition to building muscle mass, as steroids do, HGH also helps build up skeletal mass. According to Dr. William Taylor, a drug adviser to the U.S. Olympic committee, if a child were given a regimen of human growth hormone and anabolic steroids, a superathlete could result. He says it could produce a "lean 7-foot 6-inch, 350-pound athlete."

Although no athlete has been caught using human growth hormone, there are many rumors that it is being used by Olympic weight lifters, javelin throwers, and shot-putters.

Late in 1990 the FDA seized supplies of a dangerous new performance drug, gamma hydroxybutyric acid (GHB). Sold through health food stores, mail-order outlets, body building gyms, and fitness centers, GHB was claimed to release large amounts of "natural" human growth hormone during sleep to build muscle and reduce fat. But dozens of people who took it wound up in hospital emergency rooms, with symptoms including dizziness, drowsiness, vomiting, tremors, slowed heartbeat, lowered blood pressure, breathing difficulties, and coma! Drug enforcement officials expect that more alternative drugs like GHB will be coming onto the market illegally now that anabolic steroids have become tightly regulated controlled substances. "We're going after everything illegal in the anabolic steroid milieu," promises FDA attorney Michael Petty. "We're going to be very aggressive."

Blood Doping

In ancient times, warriors sometimes drank the blood of their fiercest competitors when they won in battle, thinking it would make them even more powerful. Today, some athletes are doing something similar, called blood doping (also called boosting or blood packing).

In 1976, a Finnish Olympic distance runner was accused of blood doping. He was never proven guilty, but some athletes were intrigued by the idea, and it became more popular.

The athlete freezes one or two pints of his or her own blood a few months before a race or competition. The red blood cells are replaced by the body after a short while, and the blood count returns to normal. Then, a couple of days before the race, the condensed blood is injected back into the bloodstream. Now the blood is packed with extra red blood cells. These red blood cells carry oxygen to the muscles and tissues. With more red blood cells, more oxygen can be carried, and the athlete can last longer than normal under heavy exertion before becoming exhausted. Blood doping can increase the oxygen-bearing capacity as much as 20 percent! This technique can greatly increase endurance in events like long-distance running, cycling, and skiing.

Because the added blood cells are from the athlete's own body and people's normal blood counts vary, it is very difficult to catch someone at blood doping. Athletes who use this technique run many risks, however. There is always the chance of catching an infectious disease like AIDS, hepatitis, or influenza if the athlete uses needles that aren't sterile or injects someone else's blood. Sometimes the extra red blood cells thicken the blood so much that the heart has to work harder, which could do permanent damage.

Now athletes have added another twist to blood doping. Some of them are taking EPO (erythropoietin) to increase their performance. EPO is a natural substance that stimulates the production of red blood cells. By increasing the amount of EPO in the body, athletes can stimulate an increase in their red blood cell supply. It usually will not be picked up by standard urinalysis drug testing—only a blood test will accurately detect higher levels of the substance. Possible side effects include high blood pressure and stroke. Experts believe that EPO is even more dangerous when it is combined with steroids.

HCG

Some athletes are using another natural substance called HCG or human chorionic gonadotropin. It is used medically to stimulate ovulation in women and to bring about the descent of the testes in young boys. Athletes may use this drug for several reasons. It can stimulate the production of testosterone, which makes it easier to build muscles, and it may be used to counter the breast-enlargement side effect of steroids. Ironically, supplies of black market HCG confiscated by the FDA and the Department of Justice were found not to contain the main ingredient, HCG! To make matters worse, it was found that the drug was not sterile and could cause fever and infection.

HCG comes from the urine of pregnant women. An amusing side effect is that drug tests of a male athlete who has taken HCG will indicate that he is pregnant!

Painkillers

Everyone uses painkillers like aspirin once in a while. But some athletes use powerful painkillers called narcotic analgesics that include heroin and morphine to take away pain and allow them to play harder. These types of painkillers are illegal in many countries, including the United States. Narcotics are dangerous not only because they are very addictive but also because they can cause athletes to push themselves when they are injured, which can result in more serious problems.

Anti-inflammatory Drugs

Injuries are very common in sports. Even a minor sprain or strain could sideline an athlete for days or weeks; recovering quickly could make it possible to compete in a big race or help a team in a crucial part of the season. An enthusiastic athlete might want to go on playing in spite of an injury, and coaches and trainers try to provide what help they can without risking the development of an even more serious injury.

Aspirin, ibuprofen (sold over the counter under brand names such as Advil and Nuprin), and various other NSAIDs (nonsteroidal anti-inflammatory drugs) have a double effect: they ease pain and reduce inflammation (Tylenol and other brands of acetaminophen are painkillers but do not have an anti-inflammatory effect). The painkilling effect of the NSAIDs helps athletes to ignore an injury but also may lead to further damage; but the anti-inflammatory effects help to prevent further injury. By reducing swelling, the drugs relieve the pressure on the injured tissues and aid in their healing.

The cortical steroids, such as cortisone, are the strongest anti-inflammatory drugs. They are used mainly to ease the pain of injured joints, but their short-term help may be outweighed by long-term damage. Overuse of these steroids can actually weaken the joint, resulting in further injury or the development of arthritis. Linebacker Dick Butkus successfully sued the Chicago Bears for a million dollars, claiming that the cortisone injections he had received for an injured knee resulted in permanent disability. Star pitcher Sandy Koufax had his career with the Los Angeles Dodgers cut short by severe arthritis in the elbow of his pitching arm. The cortisone injections he received while he was still pitching may have worsened the damage. A cortisone shot to help him "play through the pain" seemed like a good idea when basketball player Bill Walton suffered an injury during the 1978 NBA playoffs—but a few minutes later he had to be carried off the court. X-rays showed that without the pain warnings to guide him, he had broken a bone after the injection.

Cortical steroids can also cause hormonal problems and can make the users less able to fight off infection.

Beta Blockers

Most drugs taken by athletes are taken to give them an extra jolt of energy. They may benefit from feeling revved up and full of pep. But some athletic events require calmness, steady nerves, and delicate coordination. Some athletes may use psychological calming

Basketball player Bill Walton was a star in the 1978 NBA playoffs, as a cortisone injection helped him to "play through the pain," but it was later found that he had broken his ankle.

techniques; some may turn to alcohol or other depressant drugs. Beta blockers are also used for this purpose. There are more than a dozen different kinds of beta blockers that are normally prescribed for patients' blood pressure and heart conditions. Slowing down the heart and relieving anxiety may help to improve concentration for marksmen and pool players. But since athletes usually have average heartbeat rates, these drugs can be dangerous for them. In addition, they can be especially risky for people with asthma and diabetes.

Diuretics

Diuretics are drugs that stimulate an increase in urine production. They are prescribed for heart and kidney problems in which excess fluids build up in the body tissues, but they are sometimes used by boxers and wrestlers to help them qualify for a lower weight class without losing body muscle tissue. Some athletes also use them to mask the use of other drugs because diuretics dilute the urine. For these reasons, they are on the list of substances banned by many sports organizations. Diuretics can cause potentially dangerous side effects, including dehydration and blood disorders, as well as rashes and upset stomach.

References

Articles

Axthelm, Pete. "The Doped-Up Games." *Newsweek,* October 10, 1988, pp. 54–56.

Chelminski, Rudolph. "The Shocking Stain on International Athletics." *Reader's Digest,* August 1988, pp. 131–135.

Hecht, Annabel. "Anabolic Steroids: Pumping Trouble." *FDA Consumer,* September 1984, pp. 12–15.

Jereski, Laura. "It Gives Athletes a Boost—Maybe Too Much." *Business Week,* December 11, 1989, p. 123.

Stehlin, Dori. "For Athletes and Dealers, Black Market Steroids Are Risky Business." *FDA Consumer,* September 1987, pp. 24–25.

Taylor, William N. "Super Athletes Made to Order." *Psychology Today,* May 1985, pp. 63–66.

"Use of Blood Booster Grows Among Athletes." *Insight,* April 10, 1989, p. 53.

Books

Goldman, Bob. *Death in the Locker Room.* South Bend, Ind.: Icarus Press, 1984.

Mohun, Janet. *Drugs, Steroids, and Sports.* New York: Franklin Watts, 1988.

Wadler, Gary I., and Brian Hainline. *Drugs and the Athlete.* Philadelphia: F. A. Davis, 1989.

Pamphlets

Bartimole, John. *Drugs and the Athlete . . . a Losing Combination.* National Collegiate Athletic Association, 1988.

Newsom, Mary Margaret, ed. *Drug Free: U.S. Olympic Committee Drug Education Handbook, 1989–92.*

United States General Accounting Office. *Drug Misuse: Anabolic Steroids and Human Growth Hormone.* August 1989.

9

Are Sports Drugs Fair?

Most people think that using steroids in athletics is cheating. It gives
athletes who use them an unfair advantage over those who don't. Juan
Antonio Samaranch, president of the International Olympic Committee,
voices the opinion held by most athletic enthusiasts when he said steroid
use "makes a mockery of the very essence of sport . . . " English trainer
and sports commentator Ron Pickering declared, "We can hold athletic
endeavor in the high esteem it deserves only if we make it as clean as we
can." Olympic medical expert Dr. Robert Voy says:

> The U.S. Olympic Committee feels an obligation to the
> American public to demonstrate fair competition in amateur
> sports . . . The American public does not want to support an
> athletic program that is the best chemistry can provide; that's an
> adulterated or perverted activity. What's the point of setting
> records on pills, not innate human ability?

Most athletes—even those who use steroids—agree that athletics
would be better off without steroids. But since there are other athletes
who do use these drugs, some feel they have to use them to catch up.
They are willing to risk all the possible dangers because they believe

the drug will make the difference between being a mediocre player and a good, or great, player.

New Ethical Dilemmas

Not everyone views steroid and other performance-enhancing drugs as cheating. Some think steroids are just another technological achievement that helps an athlete to fine-tune his or her performance—like a new diet plan, better training equipment, or better running shoes.

As science becomes more and more involved in sports, the moral question of fairness is getting even fuzzier. Today's athletes have all kinds of technological advances that the athletes of yesterday didn't have. They range from video cameras that allow athletes and their trainers to point out minute changes in style that will increase performance, to specialized training equipment designed to tone up just the right muscles needed for a particular event, to devices that use electrical impulses to stimulate muscle development. "Is there that much of a difference between using a drug versus electrical impulses to stimulate muscle growth?" some would argue.

The question will undoubtedly receive even more attention as the biotechnology revolution spreads into our daily lives and doctors discover drugs and other possible performance enhancers that don't have harmful side effects. Parents and doctors already make ethical decisions in the realm of biotechnology. Growth hormones, for example, are given to children whose growth might be stunted without them. Most people would say allowing these children to receive growth hormone was a "good" decision, morally speaking.

But where do we draw the line? What about the child who will be only a mediocre basketball player no matter how hard he tries because his body will grow only to an *average* height? Some parents push their children from a very early age to excel in academics, and some push for sports. These parents may go to great lengths to "give their kid an advantage"—they may hire professional tutors or trainers, buy expensive equipment like computers or athletic gear, and instill a strong desire to compete and do well. Might some parents choose biotechnology as another tool to give their child an advantage? Why, they may argue, should their child be punished because of the physical limitations programmed into their genes?

Redefining "Natural" Ability

One of the questions that doctors, philosophers, lawmakers, and sports officials of the future will surely have to discuss is the concept of "natural abilities." Most people think it is morally unfair for athletes to take drugs that can enhance their performances. But some people think that these advances in science actually make things more fair. After all, they argue, it isn't just training that makes a great athlete. The person who is the most dedicated during training—who puts in

Sports provide an opportunity for people to develop their natural skills.

89

the most effort and the most hours—isn't always the one who wins. There are certain "natural" qualities that make the difference between a good athlete and a great athlete even when both spend the same amount of time and effort training. Some people's bodies naturally produce more or less of certain chemicals than other people's, which makes them grow more or allows them to run faster or have more energy. Some people's bodies are genetically programmed to have the potential to be bigger or stronger. Science and medicine are seen by some people as a way to even out what people have to start with.

The 1977 novel *Goldengirl,* which was later made into a movie, was about an athletic young girl who was given anabolic steroids and growth hormones to make her into a superathlete. She didn't know about the hormone treatment that went along with her training that helped win her three gold medals in the Olympic games.

This science fiction scenario could someday be reality. In fact, it could be happening today, in the United States or in other countries.

The debate about using science to extend physical limitations will undoubtedly continue. It will probably be an important question in many other aspects of society, as well. If some day, for example, scientists found a drug that wasn't harmful and could help a student to do better in school, would parents want their children to take it to help them get ahead? Would students *have* to take it just to keep up with other students who were using it? As Dr. James Wright, chief of the exercise science branch at the Army's Physical Fitness School, points out, "If there were a drug that would help professors in universities and colleges write more papers, earn more money, and get tenure, they'd all be on them."

These won't be easy questions, but for now, the majority of people in sports and the general public view performance enhancers—especially ones that are harmful to their users, like steroids—as the darker side of sports.

References

Articles

Brubaker, Bill. "Players Close Eyes to Steroids' Risks." *Washington Post,* February 1, 1987, pp. C1, C13.

Chelminski, Rudolph. "The Shocking Stain on International Athletics." *Reader's Digest,* August 1988, pp. 131–135.

Cowart, Virginia S. "Athletes and Steroids: The Bad Bargain." *Saturday Evening Post,* April 1987, pp. 56–59.

Yesalis, Charles. "Steroid Use Is Not Just an Adult Problem," *The New York Times,* December 4, 1988, p. 12.

Books

Mohum, Janet. *Drugs, Steroids, and Sports,* New York: Franklin Watts, 1988.

10

Go for It—The Right Way

Over the past few years, the attitude toward steroids has changed greatly. Coaches, trainers, and sports officials often looked the other way when it came to athletes using these drugs. Some even encouraged steroid use. But now, even among bodybuilders, where use of them has been notoriously high, steroids are being frowned upon.

Lee Haney, Mr. Olympia, is one of many musclemen heroes who have spoken out against steroids. In *Muscle & Fitness* he warned:

> You will ultimately make your best bodybuilding gains if you avoid steroid usage and just concentrate on hard training and good nutrition. But many young and impressionable body builders get on drugs within a couple of weeks or months of starting to pump iron . . . You're much better off—both in terms of health and ultimate bodybuilding gains—if you train naturally.

The keys to building a healthy body, whether you want to improve your performance in athletic events or just want to look good, are proper training, a healthy attitude about yourself and your training goals, good nutrition, and plenty of hard work.

Prize-winning bodybuilder Robert Allen started weight-lifting in college, to build up his strength for football. He enters only "natural" competitions, where all competitors take tests to prove they are free of steroids and other drugs. Allen advises the young people he works with at the Edison, New Jersey Job Corps to follow his example: "Stay clean. Be natural."

Attitude

Unfortunately, for most people in our society, the old cliché, "It's not important whether you win or lose, but how you play the game," has been replaced by "Winning isn't everything—it's the only thing." An intense competitive drive is what makes many of today's winners. For every success story, however, there are many others with the same competitive need to win who end up losers. After all, there is usually only one winner. For the people who try but fail, the competitive drive can cause a lot of problems. They may push themselves so hard that they cause or worsen injuries. They may ignore other parts of their lives—school, work, friends, or family—because of this concentration on winning. And they may resort to a win-at-all-costs attitude that leads them to try anything that might help—such as drugs like steroids.

If you want to train the right way, the first point that needs to be addressed is to reevaluate your priorities, motivations, and attitudes. Sure, you want to be the best you can and to try to improve. Competitiveness is usually considered a healthy attitude, but not when it becomes a drive to win any way you can.

Often the problem is simply one of impatience. Set small, achievable goals for yourself. When you reach them, you can reset the goal slightly higher. Don't expect to get where you want to be in a big hurry. Building up a body and improving skills take time, and troubles may start when you try to speed things up.

Training

It may be hard to keep yourself motivated for all the practice and hard work needed to excel in a sport or build a muscular body. A logbook can be a useful tool. Keeping a record of such things as body weight, muscle measurements, heart rate, as well as the amount of time training, your times or distances, or some other gauge of training activities will help you see how much progress you are making. It's hard to get a sense of progress from day to day—changes in such a short time may be too small to notice. But keeping a record allows you to see, for example, that over a period of months your time in the mile went down twenty seconds, your heartbeat slowed five beats per minute, you gained three pounds but lost an inch around the waist, gained an inch around your thigh muscles, and so on. Suddenly you realize that you really have been making good progress.

Remember that the key to effective training is to train hard enough to get results, but not so hard that you become injured.

There's only so far people can go on their own, however. Books and videos might provide some guidance, but the serious athlete will benefit most from a trainer or coach to give personal guidance. The trainer has the experience to help you determine what exercises, workouts, and other training will be needed to get to your goals. He or she may be able to point out slight mistakes and suggest changes you can make to improve your performance.

Nutrition

"You are what you eat," is one cliché that some athletes have taken a little too far. Many athletes who don't want to take drugs look instead for a "superfood" that will give them more energy and help put on muscles. There are dozens of special diets for athletes advertised in magazines. Many of them are high-protein liquid diets. Since muscle is protein, it might seem logical that eating more protein should help build muscle. But this isn't necessarily the case. In fact, most Americans eat too much protein. Exercise can help you use the proteins you eat as raw materials for building muscle tissue, but any excess protein gets stored in the body as fat.

In the opinion of most nutrition experts, the special food supplements advertised for athletes, such as brewer's yeast, bee pollen, wheat germ, ginseng, or pangamic acid, do not live up to the advertised claims, either. The key to building strong muscles and increasing energy seems to be much less glamorous—just a good well-balanced diet.

Many health experts believe the best diet is similar to the one recommended by the American Heart Association to prevent heart disease and by the National Cancer Institute to prevent cancer. In this general "good health" diet, less than 35 percent of a person's daily calories should come from fats, the most concentrated food energy source. About 50–55 percent of the daily calories should come from carbohydrates (sugars and starches), which also are used mainly for the body's energy needs. Only 15–20 percent of the daily calories need be supplied by proteins, which provide building material for growth and repair. Experts suggest that athletes should cut down even more on fats to get 55–60 percent of their calories from carbohydrates, and endurance athletes should get up to 65 percent of their calories from carbohydrates with no more than a quarter of those calories from sugars.

Vitamins and minerals are another important aspect of good nutrition. They are needed to help in the use of proteins, carbohydrates, and fats, and also in various important body reactions. Drinking plenty of liquids to replace fluids lost in sweat is also important to keep the body in prime shape.

Special Sports Diets

Normally, carbohydrates are stored as glycogen (a starch) in the muscle tissue. During exercise the contracting muscles use this glycogen as an energy source. But the body can store only a limited amount of glycogen at one time. Some athletes involved in endurance events like the marathon use a technique called carbohydrate loading to get the body to store additional glycogen, which will give them more energy during a competitive event.

About a week before an event, they increase exercise and eat a low-calorie or low-carbohydrate/high-fat diet. This will decrease the glycogen supply to the muscles. Right before the event, they eat plenty of carbohydrates and cut down on exercise. The body, starved for glycogen, will load up and store extra glycogen in the muscles. Another method of carbohydrate loading is to increase complex carbohydrates (starchy foods such as bread or pasta) for two or three days before an event.

Although carbohydrate loading can help to fine-tune a top-notch athlete, health experts advise against this practice by most people. The low-carbohydrate diet can upset the body chemistry and bring on feelings of tiredness, irritability, and muscle aches and pains. This kind of diet can also be dangerous for people with heart problems.

Many athletes place a lot of importance on the last meal they eat before an event. Experts suggest that your pre-game meal should be low in fats and protein and high in complex carbohydrates. (Fats slow down digestion, while starches provide a steady release of high-energy sugars.) The food shouldn't be too bulky to weigh you down, and most importantly, you should always leave enough time (at least several hours) to allow for digestion. Blood rushes to the stomach after eating, draining away from other organs such as the brain and muscles. (That is why you tend to feel sleepy after a big meal and also why heavy exercise right after eating can result in muscle cramps.) In addition, the body uses a lot of energy to digest food. If you engage in vigorous exercise too soon after eating, some of the needed energy will be diverted back to the muscles; the food will not be digested properly and may weigh you down.

During an endurance event such as long-distance running, cross-country skiing, or cycling, some athletes bring along fruit, bread, or other carbohydrates to give them added energy, as well as water or juice to replace lost fluids.

An unhealthy diet practice is used by some athletes (particularly wrestlers, jockeys, and boxers) who want to lose weight before an event to qualify for a lower weight class. They may either not eat before the event or eat a very low-calorie diet, or they may use diuretics, saunas, rubber suits, or other methods to try to lose water weight. These devices, however, may lead to dehydration and may place harmful stress on the heart and liver. The American College of Sports Medicine warns, "It is possible for these changes to impede normal growth and development."

Training for Sports in the Future

Sports scientists are focusing a lot of attention on nutrition as an important tool in increasing athletic performance. Researchers do not believe that the discovery of a "superfood" is likely—or desirable. Instead, they believe that athletes of the future will be monitored with frequent blood tests to check the level of nutrients before and after workouts to determine which nutrients have been used up. A computer will instantly calculate the exact diet needed for optimum performance.

Electrical stimulation of muscles may also play a role in future athletic training. Muscle contraction is normally stimulated by electrical signals, relayed by nerves. Physical therapists are experimenting with devices that apply a tiny electric current (about enough to power a night light) to muscles, stimulating vigorous contractions. In the 1988 Olympics, U.S. weight lifter Derrick Crass, who had trained with an electrical device, did

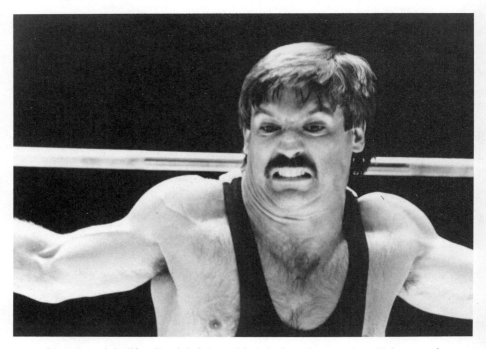

Olympic weight lifter Derrick Crass achieved a huge increase in muscle strength by training with electric stimulation.

so well that officials tested him three times for steroids. The drug tests were all negative, but researchers who studied his leg muscles found that the electrical stimulation had increased the number of muscle fibers by 13 percent. When he started training, Crass was able to lift 330 pounds in a front squat; after six weeks, he was able to lift 415 pounds—an increase of nearly half of his own 190-pound body weight!

Go for It—the Right Way

Neuromuscular electrical stimulation is still very new and controversial. (The "muscle-stimulating machines" used in gyms and health spas use a weaker current and do not stress muscles enough to build strength.) For now, the best advice for an athlete or bodybuilder is to stick to the basics: eat a well-rounded diet (low in fats and high in complex carbohydrates); drink plenty of fluids; get enough rest. To these basic health rules, add the proper training, long hours of practice, attainable goals, and the right attitude: dedication to your sport or event (without pushing so hard that you are injured) and the philosophy that you can still enjoy yourself whether you win or lose. Steroids and other drugs might seem like shortcuts, but the gains they bring may be illusions, and they come at too high a cost. Going for it the *right* way is the healthiest way to be the best you can and feel good about yourself and your body.

References

Articles

Loverock, Patricia. "Building the Athlete of the Future." *Science Digest,* September 1989, pp. 22–31.

Margen, Dr. Sheldon. "A Balanced Diet Is the Only 'Super-Food'." *Star-Ledger* (Newark, N.J.), October 23, 1988, p. 13.

"Stimulating Athletes." *Discover.* March 1989, p. 14.

Books

Goldman, Bob. *Death in the Locker Room.* South Bend, Ind.: Icarus Press, 1984.

Mohun, Janet. *Drugs, Steroids, and Sports.* New York: Franklin Watts, 1988.

Nuwer, Hank. *Steroids.* New York: Franklin Watts, 1990.

Glossary

addiction—Physical dependence on a drug or other substance, characterized by a craving for it and withdrawal symptoms when its levels in the body drop.

adrenal glands—Endocrine glands that produce a variety of hormones, including androgens.

anabolic—Pertaining to body reactions that build up tissues.

anabolic steroids—Synthetic variations of the male sex hormone, testosterone.

androgen—A general term for male sex hormones.

beta blockers—Drugs that regulate heart action.

blood doping—Injection of condensed red blood cells before a sports event.

carbohydrate loading—A training technique in which increased amounts of carbohydrates are eaten before an athletic event.

cardiovascular—Pertaining to the heart and blood vessels.

cholesterol—A naturally occurring steroid that is an essential part of cell membranes and aids in digestion but may also contribute to the buildup of fatty deposits in artery walls.

controlled substance—A drug with potential for abuse, whose prescription and use is strictly regulated (or prohibited), with violations punishable by criminal penalties.

cortisone—One of the steroid hormones produced by the adrenal glands; it has anti-inflammatory activity.

detoxification—Conversion of poisons to harmless substances.

diuretics—Drugs that stimulate urination.

doping—The taking or administration of drugs to enhance performance.

estrogen—A female sex hormone.

hormones—Chemical messengers carried through the bloodstream that help to control and coordinate body activities.

human chorionic gonadotropin (HCG)—A hormone (not a steroid) that can stimulate testosterone production.

human growth hormone (HGH)—A hormone (not a steroid) that stimulates growth and buildup of muscle and bone mass.

masculinizing effects—Increased muscular development, deepening of voice, appearance of facial hair, etc., produced by androgens.

narcotics—Painkillers related to morphine, which depress the central nervous system.

placebo effect—Effect produced when people think they are receiving a drug but actually receive an inactive substance.

random drug testing—Drug testing of members of a group selected at random, without prior notice or warning.

'roid rage—Uncontrollable fits of aggression under the influence of anabolic steroids.

"stacking"—Mixing different kinds of drugs, especially combinations of oral and injected anabolic steroids.

stanozolol—An anabolic steroid.

steroids—A class of chemical compounds, all of which contain a characteristic four-ring structure (the steroid ring system).

stimulants—Drugs that stimulate the nervous system to increase energy and alertness.

testes—The male sex glands that produce sperm and testosterone.

testosterone—A male sex hormone (chemically, a steroid).

underground lab—Unlicensed (illegal) manufacturer of drugs.

Further Reading

Articles

Altman, Lawrence. "New 'Breakfast of Champions': A Recipe for Victory or Disaster?" *The New York Times,* November 20, 1988, pp. 1, 34.

Associated Press. "Study Finds Steroids Can Cause Psychotic Symptoms Among Athletes." *Star-Ledger* (Newark, N.J.), April 1, 1988, p. 1B.

Axthelm, Pete. "Using Chemistry to Get the Gold." *Newsweek,* July 25, 1988, pp. 62–63.

————. "The Doped-Up Games." *Newsweek,* October 10, 1988, pp. 54–56.

Brody, Jane E. "Spreading Use of Steroids by Young Athletes Alarms Sports Medicine Specialists." *The New York Times,* February 18, 1988, p. B8.

Brower, Montgomery, and Carol Azizian. "Steroids Built Mike Keys Up; Then They Tore Him Down." *People,* March 20, 1989, pp. 107–108.

Brubaker, Bill. "Players Close Eyes to Steroids' Risks." *Washington Post,* February 1, 1987, pp. C1, C13.

Charlier, Marj. "Among Teen-Agers, Abuse of Steroids May Be Bigger Issue Than Cocaine Use." *Wall Street Journal,* October 4, 1988, p. A20.

Chelminski, Rudolph. "The Shocking Stain on International Athletics." *Reader's Digest,* August 1988, pp. 131–135.

Couzens, Gerald Secor. "Steroid Users Learn the Price of Success." *Star-Ledger* (Newark, N.J.), March 5, 1989, p. 11.

Cowart, Virginia S. "Athletes and Steroids: The Bad Bargain." *Saturday Evening Post,* April 1987, pp. 56–59.

Fackelmann, K. A. "Male Teenagers at Risk of Steroid Abuse." *Science News,* February 17, 1988, p. 25.

Franklin, Deborah. "Stuck on Steroids?" *In Health,* May/June, 1990, pp. 22–23.

Fultz, Oliver. " 'Roid Rage." *American Health,* May 1991, pp. 60–64.

Groves, David. "The Rambo Drug." *American Health,* September 1987, pp. 43–48.

Hecht, Annabel. "Anabolic Steroids: Pumping Trouble." *FDA Consumer,* September 1984, pp. 12–15.

Holmes, John. "Squeezing the Drugs from Athletics." *Insight,* December 26, 1988, pp. 46–47.

Jackson, Lynn M. "Steroids Are as Addictive as Any Other Drug." *Courier-News* (Bridgewater, N.J.), May 3, 1991, p. B6.

Janofsky, Michael. "System Accused of Failing Test Posed by Drugs." *The New York Times,* November 17, 1988, pp. A1, D31.

————. "Victory at Any Cost: Drug Pressure Growing." *The New York Times,* November 21, 1988, pp. 1, C13.

Jereski, Laura. "It Gives Athletes a Boost—Maybe Too Much." *Business Week,* December 11, 1989, p. 123.

Johnson, Karl. "Giants MD Lines Up on Side of Steroid Foes." *Star-Ledger* (Newark, N.J.), March 12, 1989, p. 15.

Kahler, Kathryn. "Steroids 'Mania' Spawning Perilous New Drug Traffic." *Star-Ledger* (Newark, N.J.), January 8, 1989, pp. 1, 29.

Lawn, John C. "Steroids: Playing with Trouble." *The Challenge,* November 1987, pp. 1–20.

Loverock, Patricia. "Building the Athlete of the Future." *Science Digest,* September 1989, pp. 22–31.

Margen, Dr. Sheldon. "A Balanced Diet Is the Only 'Super-Food'." *Star-Ledger* (Newark, N.J.), October 23, 1988, p. 13.

Marshall, Eliot. "The Drug of Champions." *Science,* October 14, 1988, pp. 183–184.

Maugh, Thomas H., II. "Steroid Abuse: Turning Winners into Losers." *World Book Health and Medical Annual 1990,* Chicago: World Book, 1989, pp. 42–55.

McDaniel, Jay. "Steroids in the Schools." *Star-Ledger* (Newark, N.J.), March 15, 1989, p. 16.

Miller, Roger W. "Athletes and Steroids: Playing a Deadly Game." *FDA Consumer,* November 1987, pp. 17–21.

Mirkin, Gabe. "Hormonal Helpers." *Health,* March 1984, pp. 6, 46.

Modeland, Vern. "Putting Pressure on Illegal Steroid Traffic." *FDA Consumer,* October 1989, pp. 33–34.

Penn, Stanley. "As Ever More People Try Anabolic Steroids, Traffickers Take Over." *Wall Street Journal,* October 4, 1988, p. 1.

Rowan, Carl, and David Mazie. "The Mounting Menace of Steroids." *Reader's Digest,* February 1988, pp. 133–137.

Slothower, Jodie. "Mean Mental Muscles: The Psychological Price of Steroids." *Health,* January 1988, p. 20.

Stehlin, Dori. "For Athletes and Dealers, Black Market Steroids Are Risky Business." *FDA Consumer,* September 1987, pp. 24–25.

"Stimulating Athletes." *Discover,* March 1989, p. 14.

Taylor, William N. "Anabolic Steroids." *DATAFAX Information Series,* October 1989, pp. 1–4.

———. "Super Athletes Made to Order." *Psychology Today,* May 1985, pp. 63–66.

"Teenagers Blasé About Steroid Use." *FDA Consumer,* December 1990, pp. 2–3.

Toufexis, Anastasia. "Shortcut to the Rambo Look." *Time,* January 30, 1989, p. 78.

"Use of Blood Booster Grows Among Athletes." *Insight,* April 10, 1989, p. 53.

Weaver, Warren, Jr. "U.S. Detecting Gain on Steroid Abuse." *The New York Times,* December 11, 1988, p. 35.

Yesalis, Charles. "Steroid Use Is Not Just an Adult Problem," *The New York Times,* December 4, 1988, p. 12.

Books

Goldman, Bob. *Death in the Locker Room.* South Bend, Ind.: Icarus Press, 1984.

Mohun, Janet. *Drugs, Steroids, and Sports.* New York: Franklin Watts, 1988.

Nuwer, Hank. *Steroids.* New York: Franklin Watts, 1990.

Wadler, Gary I., and Brian Hainline. *Drugs and the Athlete.* Philadelphia: F. A. Davis, 1989.

Witzmann, Rupert F. *Steroids: Keys to Life.* New York: Van Nostrand-Reinhold, 1981.

Pamphlets

American College of Sports Medicine. *Anabolic Steroids and Athletes.*

Bartimole, John. *Drugs and the Athlete . . . a Losing Combination.* National Collegiate Athletic Association, 1988.

Newsom, Mary Margaret, ed. *Drug Free: U.S. Olympic Committee Drug Education Handbook, 1989–92.*

Peterson, Robert C. *The Use of Steroids in Sports Can Be Dangerous.* National Clearinghouse for Alcohol and Drug Information, September 1988 (MS391), pp. 1–5.

United States General Accounting Office. *Drug Misuse: Anabolic Steroids and Human Growth Hormone.* August 1989.

For Further Information

American College of Sports Medicine
P.O. Box 1440
Indianapolis, IN 46206

American Council for Drug Education
204 Monroe Street
Rockville, MD 20850

Athletic Commission of New York State
270 Broadway
New York, NY 10007

The Athletics Congress (TAC)
5 West Sixty-third Street
New York, NY 10023

Department of Justice Drug Reinforcement Administration
Washington, D.C. Division
400 Sixth Street, S.W.
Washington, D.C. 20024

Drug Abuse Council, Inc.
1828 L Street, N.W.
Washington, D.C. 20036

Fair Oaks Hospital
19 Prospect St.
Summit, NJ 07901

Families in Action
National Drug Information Center, Suite 300
3845 North Druid Hills Rd.
Decatur, GA 30033

International Amateur Athletic Federation (IAAF)
3 Hans Crescent
London SW1, U.K.

International Olympic Committee (IOC)
Chateau de Vidy 1007
Lausanne, Switzerland

Just Say No Foundation
1777 North California Boulevard
Walnut Creek, CA 94596

National Basketball Assoc.
Attn: Don't Foul Out Program
645 Fifth Avenue
New York, NY 10022

National Clearinghouse for Alcohol & Drug Information
P.O. Box 2345
Rockville, MD 20852

National Clearinghouse for Drug Abuse Information
P.O. Box 416
Kensington, MD 20795

National Council on Drug Abuse
571 West Jackson Avenue
Chicago, IL 60606

National Federation of Parents for Drug-Free Youth
Suite 200
8730 Georgia Avenue
Silver Spring, MD 20910

National Hockey League
Attn: Public Relations Dept.
650 Fifth Avenue, Floor 33
New York, NY 10019

National Institute on Drug Abuse
5600 Fishers Lane
Rockville, MD 20857

New York State's Athletic Commission
270 Broadway
New York, NY 10007

Parents' Resource Institute for Drug Education (PRIDE)
Suite 1002
100 Edgewood Ave.
Atlanta, GA 30303

Public Affairs Pamphlets
381 Park Avenue South
New York, NY 10016

United States Department of Education
Attn: The Challenge Program
Reporter's Building
7th and D Streets
Washington, D.C. 20202

United States Olympic Committee
1750 East Boulder Street
Colorado Springs, CO 80909

Video Resource
"What Price Glory—The Myths and Realities of Anabolic Steroids," a 42-minute video, is available free for showing to groups and organizations from:
Dave Sinnott
Sports Science Research
35 Chester Circle, Suite 1A
New Brunswick, NJ 08901

Index

109

111

About the Authors

Dr. Alvin Silverstein is a professor of biology at City University of New York. Virginia Silverstein translates scientific Russian and is a professional author. Robert Silverstein is a graduate of Rutgers University and joined his parents writing team in 1988. The Silversteins have written a number of other important books for young people, including *AIDS: Deadly Threat*, and *The Addictions Handbook*.